kids
who can
concentrate

01818

Also by Jean Robb and Hilary Letts

CREATING KIDS WHO CAN
CREATING KIDS WHO CAN PASS EXAMS

Creating
kids
who can
concentrate

Proven strategies for beating
ADD **without** drugs

Jean Robb & Hilary Letts

HODDER
MOBIUS

Hodder & Stoughton

Copyright © 1997 by Jean Robb and Hilary Letts

First published in 1997 by Hodder Headline Australia Pty Limited
First published in Great Britain in 1997 by Hodder and Stoughton
First published in paperback in 2002 by Hodder and Stoughton
A division of Hodder Headline

The right of Jean Robb and Hilary Letts to be identified as the Authors of
the Work has been asserted by them in accordance with the Copyright,
Designs and Patents Act 1988.

1 3 5 7 9 10 8 6 4 2

A CIP catalogue record for this title is available from the British Library

ISBN 0 340 82044 6

Printed and bound in Great Britain by
Mackays of Chatham plc, Chatham, Kent

Hodder & Stoughton
A division of Hodder Headline
338 Euston Road
London NW1 3BH

About the authors

Jean Robb is an inspirational teacher. She has worked in many countries unravelling the mysteries of learning for parents and their children. Her holistic methods take away the barriers to learning that limit potential.

In 1990 she teamed up with children's librarian and teacher Hilary Letts to form the education foundation, Successful Learning.

As educational therapists, Jean and Hilary work with people who have barriers to learning. These include people who are very bright but disorganised; who have behavioural difficulties; who are wanting to overcome a weakness – academically or socially; who have suffered trauma; who have a physical difficulty or who need help in a particular subject. They also include people who don't know how to learn effectively; who panic; who have been labelled as having learning difficulties; who want to learn techniques for success in exams. Jean and Hilary also work with parents who have met a barrier when helping their children.

This book has grown out of more than 32 years experience in teaching children of every age and ability, and in dealing with their parents.

Now Jean and Hilary enable all children, even those labelled dull, lazy, naughty, difficult or remedial, to astound themselves and startle their teachers by making good the damage of years of missed lessons, misunderstood lessons and mixed messages.

Jean and Hilary also work with gifted children to liberate them from the stress of being super-bright, especially gifted or multitalented, by showing them the way of realising their own potential, preventing them from becoming bored and allowing them to celebrate their gifts.

In addition to their work with children, Jean and Hilary also run courses for parents, adults with barriers to learning, and people who are experiencing stress, work difficulties or behavioural difficulties.

Jean and Hilary's practical tips are appreciated by readers of the parenting pages in the *Guardian* and in other publications for parents.

He/She

Parents of boys and parents of girls worry about their children's concentration.

We use he in one chapter and she in the next in this book, so that all parents can see that the problems are not confined to boys.

Contents

Part III

Effective Parenting 169

How to use this book

Begin at the beginning and read through chapter by chapter to understand why we say:

1. Effective concentration matters to every child.
2. Effective concentration must be taught to every child.
3. You can teach your child to concentrate effectively.

The book has been organised into three parts. The first part shows how lack of concentration has come to be called a medical condition. Medical condition or not, when you take into consideration the ways children are taught and live today, it becomes easy to devise techniques to help them learn to concentrate.

The second part takes you through a series of case studies. These illustrate the types of problems that cause concern and suggest some solutions. Like any good Do-It-Yourself manual, once you master the basic techniques, you become confident about devising solutions to suit your child and your life.

The third part shows how adults helping children can help each other as well as themselves. This part includes suggestions that can be used by support groups and schools as well as parents. Use the relaxations in (see page 228) to give you a tranquil moment as you work your way through the book.

By the end of the book, you will find that you have increased your understanding of how children become good at concentrating, and you will have developed techniques to teach your child to concentrate. This knowledge will give you a firm base to build on whenever you see or hear a talk or discussion on the problems of concentration.

PART I
What does
concentration
mean?

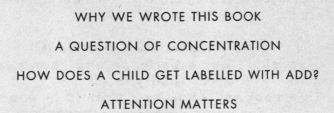

Why we wrote this book

Parents want and need to know how to help their children. We have worked for many years with children who can't concentrate including children who have been labelled as having ADD. We have worked with parents and teachers to show them what they can do about it.

**We have written this book
to share our experience and knowledge
with you.
This book will show you that it is possible
for you to work successfully
with children who can't concentrate
and transform them into
children who can concentrate.**

This book will show you how to find solutions.

- Solutions can be found when you adopt a holistic approach.
- Solutions can be found when you recognise the small improvements. Small improvements always lead to giant leaps forward.

Using our holistic approach you can transform children. The unlovable will become lovable, the noisy will become calm, the clumsy will become careful, the impulsive will become thoughtful and the forgetful will begin to remember.

You can take children with low self esteem and watch them grow in confidence, assurance and awareness of others.

You can take the reckless and help them overcome the cause of their recklessness because they learn to relax and find other ways of dealing with stressful situations or their need for excitement.

You can take children who have never had a friend and help them find ways of speaking and behaving which will open the door and allow friendship to grow.

You can take children who have experienced only the despair rather than the delight of those who love them and turn them into valued companions who are a joy to be with and whose progress is a source of wonder to all who know them.

You can beat the barriers to understanding.

We have done it again and again and know you can do it too. Bringing about the transformation takes time and energy. It's easy to think sometimes you are getting it wrong. Keep believing in your own ability to succeed and keep referring to the experiences we describe in our book and you will find solutions that work for you and your child.

A HOLISTIC APPROACH INVOLVES FINDING OUT:

- Why your child is saying or doing something which seems wrong or peculiar.
- When your child manages well at home or at school.
- What your child needs to feel well—sleep, food, rest, play, friends.
- How your child can help—everyone needs to feel they are part of what is happening.
- Who your child is copying—a television character, a friend, a classmate or a relative.
- What your child finds frightening, sad, funny or comforting.
- Whether your child knows when he is upsetting somebody.
- Why your child thinks it is all right to behave badly. He will have a reason, but until you find it, although he will have improved in many situations, sometimes it will feel as if he has gone back to square one.
- How to develop ways to help your child deal with the real world.

When you use a holistic approach, you will be more likely to find a solution because you will find that you can think more clearly.

Our work shows that adults have most success when they don't give up. In our work we focus on overcoming barriers to understanding because we believe that:

- barriers to understanding stop children from achieving their full potential
- barriers to understanding prevent adults from seeing how they can help children reach their full potential

What are the barriers to understanding?

Some barriers to understanding are:

1. Not knowing what is expected.
2. Not knowing how to do what is expected.
3. Being frightened of doing what is expected, and protecting yourself by doing something else instead.
4. Thinking you understand what you are expected to do, and not realising that there is still something else to learn.
5. Thinking that what you are being asked to do is easy, and not realising that you will need to think about what is involved and plan carefully how to do it.

There are others.

We have found that some children who can't concentrate have no idea of the way they appear to other people. This is a very significant barrier to understanding because these children think that everything that happens to them is random, unfair or inexplicable.

Children can learn, however, to understand the effect their behaviour has on other people. They can learn that:

- the way they treat others
- the way they behave in front of others
- the way they work with others

have consequences.

Children learn that the best consequences will give them most options. They can learn how to think about other people. They can learn how to make other people want to be with them and help them. When they have learned this, children who have been disruptive, disagreeable and disappointing, will behave well at home, at school and at play.

A question of concentration

SORRY I WAS MILES AWAY ... WHAT DID YOU SAY?

There are times when we all find it difficult to concentrate. Sometimes it is difficult because:

- we have too much on our minds
- we have too many other distractions or worries
- we don't know how to do what we're supposed to be doing
- we want to do something else
- the person we're supposed to be listening to is droning on and on
- we are tired
- we are not feeling well
- we have eaten or drunk too much—or too little
- we have eaten the wrong thing

Most of the time when we realise we are not concentrating we sort it out. We have lots of ways of doing this. We might talk to a friend about what's bothering us, go to bed and catch up on our sleep, find somewhere quiet, have something to eat or drink or make a list of what needs to be done and ask someone how to do it.

Children find it difficult to concentrate for the same reasons that adults do. They get tired, feel hungry, are worried about things or need a break. Children often don't have enough experience or control over their own lives to sort out the things that are stopping them from concentrating—sometimes they don't even know what is stopping them from concentrating.

Why, when we all have difficulty concentrating sometimes, are children who can't concentrate sometimes labelled as having ADD?

We demand a great deal from children today—but sometimes we forget to teach them what they have to do or how they have to behave to meet those demands. Concentration is one such demand. If children can't concentrate we give them a label. One such label is ADD.

The ADD label is currently given to children and adults who, when tested and interviewed, seem unable to conform to the social and academic expectations considered normal for their age and ability. Today the number of children labelled as having ADD is growing in epidemic proportions.

Children may be labelled as having ADD if they:

- can't organise
- disrupt other people
- bite, kick and scream
- can't make eye contact
- have trouble understanding consequences
- are easily bored
- have no fear
- are impatient
- are impulsive
- experience mood swings
- are insecure
- have poor self esteem
- are restless
- have a short attention span

We have found with our holistic approach to teaching that we can help children overcome or improve all these ways of behaving. We find out where the child has a gap in understanding or needs some support, and once we fill the gaps and support the child, the behaviour improves.

What Are the Gaps in Understanding?

Gaps in understanding are when there's a vital piece of information missing and the missing piece prevents the child from using the rest of the knowledge he does have. He can't make something work, he can't cope with a situation, he can't get the right answer even when he tries hard. Gaps in understanding leave children feeling confused and hopeless.

HOW HAVE GAPS IN UNDERSTANDING DEVELOPED?

SOME PEOPLE SAY:
It is because of stress on families
Children and families have always had traumas. Parents have died, families have split up, people have lost their jobs, families have had to build new lives in unfamiliar places.

It is because of environmental stresses
The lives of children and their families have frequently been disrupted by illness and poor health, poor housing conditions, pollution.

It is because of computers, television and videos
Technological change is not new. The lives of children and their families have always been affected by technological change.

It is because adults forget what it is like to be a child
The generation gap has long caused parents to shake their heads in despair, disbelief or amazement.

It is because of working parents
Children have always had to adjust to being looked after by different people on occasion, depending on what was happening in their lives and in their families at the time.

It is because there are so many experts
Parents have always turned to other people with more experience to help them be good parents.

It is because parents are too anxious
There have always been parents who wanted to do the best for their children.

It is because of new teaching techniques
Children have regularly had to cope with new fads in learning in the education system.

It is because children have too much fun

Children, even those who were pushed up chimneys, have always had entertainment as part of their lives. Many children used to create their own entertainment.

It is because advertisers exploit children and their parents

Children have always been attracted by novelties and have always been prepared to encourage their parents to help them get what they want.

It is because children aren't given responsibility

In the past children were given responsibility. If the responsibility was too great their school work might suffer, but they would still learn skills to help them deal with life and develop concentration. If responsibility is at the right level, children will be well equipped for adulthood. We believe that when children are encouraged and educated to take responsibility for their own behaviour and to realise that they are capable of learning and being adaptable, they will benefit from the help that they are given. They will know that gaps in understanding are part of life. They will learn how to fill in the gaps.

TAKING RESPONSIBILITY

Some children are not given the support and understanding they need to take on responsibilities. Without responsibility children will only concentrate when they want to. Children need to be given responsibility so they will understand about consequences. A child with no idea about consequences is frustrating to deal with. In the current climate it has become easier to decide there is something wrong with the child rather than find ways of teaching the child how to have a sense of responsibility and therefore an understanding of consequences.

Responsibilities you can give children

We believe that when children are taught to take responsibility for their own behaviour, they will realise that they are capable of learning. They won't need drugs to become adaptable and will benefit from the teaching that they are given. Here are some responsibilities you can give children.

- Looking at the person who is speaking to you is a fundamental responsibility and children need to be taught that it is important and how to do it.
- Asking permission before using something new or something that belongs to someone else.
- Tidying up.
- Setting the table for meal times.
- Taking the rubbish out.

SO, WHY IS THERE AN OUTBREAK OF ADD?

The term ADD is used to describe children who behave in particular ways. Most often it is used to describe children with poor concentration and a short attention span.

There are undeniably many people of all ages and abilities who don't know how to concentrate. But this, on its own, doesn't mean they have ADD. It may simply mean that they have never learned how to concentrate. Concentration can be taught. For children to learn concentration, they must be given responsibility, must feel that their contribution to family life matters and must have the chance gradually to develop the skills everyone needs in order to be able to function successfully. Once this is done, they will no longer be disorganised, impulsive, restless, withdrawn or cause their parents and teachers to be justifiably worried. If the real reason for this worrying behaviour isn't recognised, they are in danger of being labelled as having ADD.

In some children, ADD may be a medical problem. But even for these children we do not believe that medication such as Ritalin, Tefranil, Cylert, Dexedrine, Elavel or Norpramin, is the only answer.

ADD or ADHD?

Where children have an inability to focus and concentrate, they may be described as having ADD. Where children have an inability to focus, concentrate or sit still they may be described as having ADHD. In this book we have only used the term ADD, although the methods suggested are successful for people who are diagnosed as having ADHD or are simply exuberant or scatty.

What we say about ADD

Much has been written about what ADD is and the best ways of treating it. Some experts believe in modifying behaviour, some in controlling diet and some in using drugs such as Ritalin.

In a society which teaches children to say 'no' to mood altering drugs, we think that using drugs to alter a child's behaviour gives worrying messages to a vulnerable group.

We believe that the danger for children being given drugs to calm them down is that they come to believe that they do not have to take responsibility for their own actions. They begin to believe they will always have to use the drug when they want to learn anything or behave reasonably. For these children, the pride in learning self control, self discipline and new skills for new stages of life has been taken away. Any improvement is seen to be as a result of the drug, not the child's learning or increased understanding.

WHAT HAPPENS WHEN YOUR CHILD CAN'T CONCENTRATE?

A child who fails to concentrate in one situation is in danger of being seen as a child who can't concentrate in any situation. If a child doesn't sit still he is in danger of being called hyperactive. His parents might be panicked into believing hyperactivity and poor concentration are permanent conditions which will need specialist treatment. This treatment might include medication.

In the past, concentration and being still were skills children were taught. Where many activities compete for the time available, the teaching of those skills can be delayed and possibly missed altogether. This can happen in any family and at any time. The discussion about ADD means that when a lack of concentration becomes a problem, it is assumed it is a medical condition. People do not realise that the child has not been taught how to concentrate.

Concentration is a skill that parents and teachers can teach. Once concentration is learnt most children can operate successfully. Children who learn to concentrate are not boring. Children who concentrate still have individual characteristics. Being an individual is not a problem providing your individuality doesn't cause someone else a problem.

How you can check on your child's concentration

You can check whether your child can concentrate by giving him something to do which he enjoys doing, and which takes concentration. If your child can pay attention to the activity for at least five minutes you will know he can concentrate. If your child's attention wanders, before five minutes is up, maybe he does need your help.

How you can help a child who can't concentrate

Some children seem to be able to concentrate better than others. But, if you only ever compare one child against other children, you may miss noticing important information about an individual child's progress and development.

Remember that children are all different.

It is important to focus on the individual child. It is important to compare what the child is doing this week with what he was doing last week; how he behaved when he went to bed tonight compared with how he behaved when he went to bed last night; how he played with other children at the park compared with how he plays with them at home.

When you focus on the individual and notice changes in that child's behaviour it helps you to avoid becoming trapped into thinking that a child has an insurmountable problem simply because the child is different from others.

Why it is important to be wary of checklists for ADD

Checklists can make you feel they are describing unusual behaviours, but often they are only describing things that every child will do sometimes.

Checklists can reinforce the feeling that your child has a difficulty which only experts can help to sort out.

Checklists can convince you that your child has a medical condition.

Checklists can be so all inclusive that a parent or teacher who is worried about a child will find something on the list that applies to that child.

Checklists for ADD can include these questions:

- Does your child forget instructions?
- Does your child have a short temper?
- Does your child fidget?
- Does your child constantly ask questions?
- Does your child move in a clumsy way?
- Does your child produce messy written work?
- Does your child leave his bedroom untidy?
- Does your child suffer from mood swings?

For some parents and teachers, this simply looks like a list of the stages that all children go through and outgrow They will not be worried, but at the same time they might think carefully about some particular problems to find a way to help the child move ahead.

What you can do once you've seen a checklist

If as a result of seeing the list you think that your child's difficulties come from a medical problem, you may decide to see a doctor because you feel that medication is the answer in this situation. You may even worry that it would be negligent not to get medication.

Alternatively, if you think that your child has a learning problem, then you can work with him to sort it out. By paying attention to what your child is doing, you will find ways to help him overcome the problem.

What do we do when we see a child whom everyone thinks can't concentrate?

When we see a child whom everyone says can't concentrate we ask those who are worried some questions.

We always ask if there is ever a time when the child can concentrate. Sometimes people are so worried that they can't think of anything at all. We give them a prompt. We ask them if the child can concentrate:

- playing football
- dancing
- watching television
- playing on the computer
- talking to friends
- reading comics
- playing with a younger child
- making something with building blocks like Lego
- drawing
- colouring in
- writing
- doing a puzzle
- playing with a toy
- playing with the family pet

We point out that if someone can concentrate in one situation, then the problem is not an inability to concentrate. The problem could be that the child does not know how to ask for help and switches off or the child does not know how to do something, but nobody has realised that he needs help.

Secondly, if no one can think of a time when the child has ever concentrated, we give the child an activity to do—building with blocks, a jigsaw, spelling, to see if concentration is possible. It invariably is.

Our approach is holistic.
It does not use medication.

We believe that a holistic approach is important because it helps all children even if the problem is a medical one and not just a lack of understanding. A holistic approach helps children learn how to develop their strengths and in so doing reduces the effect their medical condition or their lack of understanding has on their behaviour.

QUESTIONS PARENTS ASK THEMSELVES

Am I to blame?
No. There are so many influences in a child's life that it is impossible even for the most caring parent to protect their children from every difficult situation. It is also impossible to predict which situation a child will find difficult and which situation he will find easy.

Some experts say that since ADD is a medical condition there can be absolutely no blame attached to parents. We agree that no blame should be attached to parents when a child cannot concentrate or is diagnosed as having ADD.

However, we believe that parents can do a great deal to help a child learn to concentrate.

- If you pay attention to your child, give eye contact and answer questions you will be showing your child how to concentrate.
- If you insist that your child gives you eye contact when asking you a question or telling you about his day, you will be helping him learn skills for concentration.

**A holistic approach
helps children learn how to
develop their strengths.**

The A to Z of Improving Concentration

Ask him to tell you how the day was for him.

Breakfast that is sensible will start the day well for him.

Change—help him understand how to cope with his fear of change.

Decisions—help him understand how decisions take time.

Energy—going for walks, swimming or playing with a ball will release pent-up energy for both of you.

Foot massage.

Go at his pace sometimes and teach him how to go at your pace as well.

Handwriting practice helps self esteem.

Involve him by pointing out how a particular incident affected other people around him. Make sure you tell him when he has done something good as well as something bad.

Jigsaw puzzles help with organisation.

Knowledge—learning something new takes time.

Listen to him and he will learn how to listen to you.

Make sure he is clean and his clothes are clean when he leaves the house.

Notice when things are going well.

Organise your life so that the family doesn't become the victim of one member.

Provide a consistent approach to the way you deal with him. If you change it, explain why.

Quality time is important.

Relaxation before bedtime will help.

Speak politely and your child will learn from you.

Teach him to rule straight lines.

Understand the importance of his doing jobs around the house.

Value your efforts and his—don't give up.

Worthwhile effort gives pleasure—give him a chance to find that out.

e**X**plore your local environment with him and he will feel involved with his community.

Young people need time, teaching and tasks.

Zest—create a situation where your child's exuberance, energy and creativity are developed in such a way that he and everyone he comes into contact with will be delighted.

Why are some children so impossible?

Parents are confused when one child in the family causes difficulty. They say, 'All my children were brought up the same way so there must be something wrong with this one because he is so different from his brothers and sisters.'

Every child is individual. It is important to remember that no two children are ever brought up in the same way—even in the same family. Just being born into a different position in the family means one child will have a different experience from another. Having chickenpox at a particular time in a school career can be a different experience for one child from his brothers and sisters. A house move can mean one child can make friends easily and another can find no one available. As a result one child may become confident yet the other become a lonely child uncertain of his ability to make friends.

'What can I do? I am at my wit's end'

Children and parents benefit when children are helped to find ways of overcoming their difficulties. It can be a waste of time looking for someone or something to blame. Of course there will always be a reason why the child is having difficulty. But, you may never find the reason. Don't worry. Even if that reason isn't found, you can still help the child find ways to overcome his problem.

Parents often feel guilty when they are cross or fed up with their children. They feel that they have let themselves down and may then resent the child because he's not perfect and therefore they can't be perfect parents. Many parents have felt this way. However, it is worth learning to be patient. You learn so much about yourself when you have to think of other ways of sorting out a problem rather than getting angry. You will not always succeed. Do not criticise yourself or your child. Notice what happened, practise relaxation and you will gradually find ways of overcoming the problem.

You can do it.

By paying attention to how your child feels, you can find out if your child is unhappy, uncomfortable or unsure. This is a good place to start to find ways you can help.

The most important thing to do is to keep reminding yourself and your child that there are things he does which are all right and things he does which are not. When he behaves well he is welcome in any group. When he is behaving badly he is unwelcome. Remind him of things he has learned successfully and reassure him he will learn to do even more things successfully.

Giving children unreal expectations that let them think that they have a 'condition' that will be indulged in later life is unfair. To lead happy and fulfilling lives and achieve their potential, children have to learn how to conform across the normal range of behaviour that is tolerated in society. That normal range is quite wide.

We all know adults who are leading successful lives today who might have been seen as children with special needs, if giving children who couldn't concentrate labels had been the fashion, when they went to school. Although it is essential to understand what the problems and difficulties are, labels do not always help. People with disabilities will confirm that. Even though the law is supposed to protect their rights to employment, adulthood is a struggle for people with disabilities and they have to learn how to cope with difficulties they meet, often on a daily basis.

Every child is individual.

How to Teach Your Child to Concentrate

You can learn how to teach your child to concentrate, when he needs to. The basics are simple.

YOU NEED TO:
- Give time and thought to what you want to teach.
- Use mistakes as an opportunity to learn—whether you make them or your child makes them.
- Accept that while your child is learning from you, you can be learning from your child. By observing what your child does, you can learn how your child learns and learn how to help your child be successful.
- Give your child a chance to practise the skill you teach.
- Give your child feedback on what has been done well and what needs further work.

YOU CAN:
Show your child how to use what he knows
Just because your child concentrates in one situation, it does not mean he will automatically be able to concentrate in every situation.

Build your child's concentration step by step
If your child can't concentrate in one situation that doesn't mean he or she won't ever be able to concentrate.

Find out what your child needs to learn
If your child is not concentrating at home maybe he or she doesn't know how to do what you want.

Fill the gap in understanding
If your child is concentrating at home but not at school maybe there is some situation at school which is making concentration difficult. There could be a gap between the demands being put on your child and what he or she knows.

Learn by paying attention
Don't forget the best teaching comes when you are all learning.

THE CHILD WHO KEPT HER EYES ON THE BALL
AND THE PARENTS WHO KEPT THEIR EYES ON THE CHILD.

Tracy went to a tennis match with her parents. They had spent a lot of money buying a ticket for her and wanted her to enjoy tennis as much as they did. They hoped going to tennis tournaments would become a family activity. They were disappointed as they watched Tracy because she didn't appear to be taking any interest in the game. In fact, what Tracy was watching was the ball boys. She hadn't been told where to look while the game was happening. She didn't realise that the game which she should have been watching, was between the two people holding the rackets. She thought the game was the ball boys racing after the balls. When the game finished Tracy chatted enthusiastically to her parents about what she had seen. Only then did they understand that far from not concentrating she had absorbed a great deal from the game she had been watching. Their disappointment changed into delight as they realised that there was a logic to what she had been doing. They also learned that next time they took her to something new, they couldn't assume she would automatically know what to expect or how to behave.

Tracy was lucky. Her parents quickly realised why she wasn't concentrating on the tennis players. Instead of getting cross with her, or not taking her to any more tournaments, they appreciated her logic and then explained to her that there was another game she could look at—the one between the two people holding rackets!

Tracy's parents paid attention. They asked Tracy how she had enjoyed the game. They could have listed all the disappointing things they had noticed about her behaviour. Instead, they gave her time to explain her logic.

If Tracy's parents had thought she was unable to pay attention, they may have gone to an expert for help. An expert, not realising Tracy had misunderstood the game, may have thought she had a problem and given her a label.

How does a child become labelled with ADD?

WHAT TESTS TELL YOU

WHAT IS A LABEL?

HOW DO LABELS COME ABOUT?

WHY DO WE LABEL OUR CHILDREN?

PARENTS AS CUSTOMERS

WHAT ALTERNATIVES ARE THERE TO LABELS?

At some point in a child's development, what he wants to do will clash with what you or someone else want him to do. Your child may only ever do what he wants and ignore what you need him to do. The gap between what your child wants to do and what you want him to do may worry you and other adults very much and everybody begins to hunt for a solution.

- An aunt reads an article about children with ADD and says this sounds just like her niece who never concentrates on anything.
- A grandmother sees a television program on children who can't concentrate and thinks it is just like her grandson who is always forgetting things.
- A teacher goes on an in-service training course and thinks one of his pupils must have ADD because he is so disruptive.
- Dad meets a friend at the club whose son has been diagnosed as having ADD and he thinks that the problems sound just like the ones his own son has.
- A doctor suggests that a child is taken to an expert on ADD because he is becoming violent.

What Tests Tell You

When parents and teachers become worried about a child's behaviour, the child may be taken to be tested. Tests always need to be treated with caution. It is important to understand that test results do not always tell you what a child can really do. They just tell you what the person who constructed the test thinks she can do.

If your child is being given a set test, the person administering the test has to follow the special procedure that has been established for that test. Sometimes, when the procedure is followed, important pieces of information about what a child can do may be missed.

**It is important to understand
that test results do not always tell you
what a child can really do.**

EMMA AND THE MISSING LINK

Emma was being tested by an expert. One of the questions was to find out whether she could understand the link between two words. The question was, 'What is the link between blue and green?' Emma said that both the words had the letter 'e'. The only answer that could be accepted by the test, was: 'they are both colours'. The standard test did not allow for Emma's individual logic and answer.

Even observation does not always tell you what the child can really do. You must look at the inconsistencies in the child's behaviour and look for the explanation.

TOM WAS NOISY WHEN HE WAS IGNORED

Tom was taken to see an expert on ADD. While he was in the consulting room he crawled on the floor, opened the doctor's briefcase and stopped any chance of a sensible conversation by making a lot of noise. No one asked Tom to stop. His behaviour was noted and the diagnosis was given as ADD. What the doctor had really observed was that sometimes Tom misbehaved when he was ignored.

WHAT IS A LABEL?

A label describes what the person does or doesn't do. It doesn't really describe who the person is. The people who give labels are usually 'experts'. In this book we describe 'experts' as anyone who gives an opinion.

Some experts have special training and qualifications and specialise in child development. They may also have power (the doctor, teacher, health visitor) and their opinions will go on a child's record. Other 'experts' are the people whose opinion you respect and value because of their experience and common sense, and who influence you or your child even though their opinion is never written down. These experts may be family members, such as an aunt, neighbour, or grandparent, friends, neighbours or colleagues.

What is wrong with a label?

Unfortunately labels are too often used as if they describe the whole person rather than just a characteristic.

'Meet Mike, he's dyslexic.'

'My son is ADD.'

'Sally is a dyspraxic child.'

Labels tend to put a child into a category from which it can be almost impossible to escape. The child then comes to see himself as a person with a permanent condition rather than someone, who, if he puts in the effort, will be able to change and grow and learn:

- how to read
- how to organise
- how to pay attention
- how to make eye contact
- how to speak clearly
- how to be still and wait

What happens when you've got the label?

The danger in labelling children is that whenever an adult is dealing with a child with a label, the adult may think everything he does must take account of the child's label.

- Anything the child does which shows he has a problem reinforces the label.
- Anything which shows the child has more potential than initially thought is ignored or treated as a fluke.

Catch 22 and all that!

A child may be given help and offered a place in a rigorous and structured program, which goes along step-by-step at a pre-determined pace. If he develops much faster than the program allows, that achievement isn't recognised.

Alternatively, a child can end up with no help to teach him how to overcome the problem, because his condition is seen as needing specialist help but there's no specialist available. In this situation, people use the label to explain his lack of achievement.

Are labels new?

Labels are not new. There have always been labels. We all use them. Children miss opportunities because they are called:

- slow
- thick
- flat footed
- a child from an unsupportive family

Children receive opportunities because they are called:

- bright
- well mannered
- helpful
- a child from a supportive family

Are all children with the ADD label viewed in the same way?

Children with an ADD label are all different and have characteristics that affect people in different ways.

Sometimes a child who irritates and gets the ADD label, is attractive, cute or can tell a good story. The attractiveness is seen as a fortunate characteristic by some. Although attractiveness won't compensate for the fact he can't sit still, this good quality will make his behaviour seem tolerable.

Sometimes a child who irritates and is labelled ADD is unattractive, naughty and almost impossible to communicate with. The unattractiveness is seen as an unfortunate characteristic by some. The unattractive child hasn't those qualities which make him tolerable to others. Without help, he will not become a person other people want to be with.

For both children, being tolerable or intolerable won't mean the label changes or that they will have learnt to sit still. In fact, they may believe they are people who can't be the same as everyone else. They may have worked out what people are expecting and practise that behaviour. This strategy stops them from learning anything that requires work because the minute they feel pressure, they switch to their 'cute' or 'strange' behaviour.

Why don't labels help?

Labels don't help because there is no guarantee the support given will help overcome the condition. In fact, it might do the opposite, and make it worse.

- Just because the support worked for one child, doesn't mean that it is right for every child.
- Just because the support worked once on a particular child, it doesn't mean it is going to work every time for that child.

**Labels tend to put a child
into a category from which
it can be almost impossible to escape.**

HOW DO LABELS COME ABOUT?

Labels usually start describing people who are sharing the same interest or lifestyle or difficulty. If these labels for people take on a derogatory tone, at some point there may be a reaction to them.

A language is constantly changing. Some labels are eliminated because at different times the terms become offensive. Many people lead single lives and the labels spinster, bachelor and old maid are rarely used now because they are seen as dated or offensive.

In the UK, the Spastic Society changed it's name to Scope. Scope is described as a charity to support people with cerebral palsy. The charity recognised the old label meant that the people they were supporting were being limited by being described as spastic, and nothing else. The individuals were only being described by their medical condition not their human condition.

Many individuals are no longer prepared to lump or be lumped into a group. They are not prepared to accept a situation where there is no difference made between the people, because there is no recognition that each person is unique.

The word 'scope' carries the feeling of possibilities—possibilities for the people with the condition and possibilities for those who meet them, work with them or live with them.

Which labels do we need?

Labels can be useful. Some labels describe the work we do. In the workplace we need to know who does what. When we go into hospital we need to know who is the doctor and who is the nurse. If we are making a complaint about service, we need to know the difference between the sales assistant and the manager.

- Labels can help communication when they tell us who does what.
- Labels can destroy communication when they restrict our knowledge of all the capabilities of a person.

We all use labels and are labelled

What labels do people use when they talk about you? Are you a mother, old, young, helpful, a colleague, a friend? Are you artistic, sporty, disabled, fascinating, meticulous? Are you serious, clumsy or cheerful? Are you an optimist or a pessimist? When we talk about people we often use labels to describe them, but we know it is only a label and not the whole person.

When 'experts' talk about people, they use labels as a shorthand to describe a condition. Sometimes one of these labels becomes fashionable and suddenly lots of people are using it to describe people. It is these labels that can limit the way we see people and become a barrier to understanding.

Changing language

We use new words often. Some words are only fashionable for a short time. Some are only fashionable in particular groups.

- Teenagers use new words, and old words in new ways, as part of their development. Language is one of the things that they have control over and can experiment with.
- Experts use new words and old words in new ways. We can feel unable to join in the discussion properly because we don't understand what the experts' language means.

**When words are used to describe
your child's behaviour
make sure the words really describe
your child's behaviour.**

These days, while we are energetically rejecting labels that stereotype people because we realise how limiting they are, we are still lumping children with problems or difficulties together under coverall labels like ADD.

WHY DO WE LABEL OUR CHILDREN?

'I've been told children will get help once they have a label.'

Parents and labels
Parents are often bewildered when their child does not develop in the way they expect, or does not develop like other children. When their child is described as ADD, they are often relieved to find that they are not alone, that at last someone understands their problems and that there is a way of describing the child's problems or a reason that explains the child's behaviour.

Parents who feel comfortable with labels
Some parents feel that the label does explain their child's behaviour and is the most effective way of getting help. They may have been frustrated in the past when they tried unsuccessfully to get help for their child. They believe that now the problem is identified, everything will be all right and the child will receive the extra teaching or extra help needed.

Parents who feel uncomfortable with labels
Other parents do not want their child to have a label. They fear that a label may carry a stigma that disadvantages their child and possibly condemn him to a second-rate education, reducing his opportunities for fulfilling his potential.

If you are unhappy with the label, keep looking for answers elsewhere. Don't be pushed.

Labels aren't all they are cracked up to be!

Once a child has a label, most parents expect their child will at last receive the specialist teaching he needs. Parents may have different expectations about what the special teaching will achieve. Some parents will expect teaching to support the problem and others will expect it to overcome the problem.

Unfortunately, sometimes no special teaching or support is offered at all. At this point a parent's frustration and sense of powerlessness can increase their anxiety and lead to frantic efforts on behalf of the child.

Once you are in such an anxious position, you have a range of options.

YOU CAN:
- Join a support group.
- Set up your own support group.
- Take your child to another medical expert.
- Take your child to another psychological expert.
- Take your child to another psychiatric expert.
- Take your child to a hypnotist.
- Take your child to an alternative health practitioner.
- Go on a course yourself.
- Read a book.

PARENTS AS CUSTOMERS

Parents of children having difficulties are vulnerable. If you are in this position, consider the following points carefully before you make any decisions.

'I think I'll go to an expert!'

There are experts who can help you and your child. Whenever you go to any expert you have to allow a little leeway for the individual style of the expert. However, do not sign up for anything on the spot. It is sensible to go away and think about it first. You are there to find out whether that expert is going to help you and your child.

FIND OUT FROM THE EXPERT:
- How much is it going to cost?
- What do you get for your money?
- How long will you or your child be signed up for?
- What are the add-on costs?
- What do you have to pay up-front?
- Is there anyone who has had success using the program? (By success make sure you are asking about solutions and not whether the program is enjoyable, expensive or fashionable.)

ASK YOURSELF:
- Does the expert seem to understand me?
- Does the expert seem to understand the individual nature of my child's problem?
- Does the expert seem to have one standard response?
- Why am I doing this?
- What could be the problems with this method?
- Do I think this expert is talking common sense or am I being blinded with science/psychology?
- Am I being treated as if I can think?
- Is the space my child will have to visit child friendly?
- Is the expert blaming or explaining?
- Have I been asked what I know about my child?
- How much feedback will I get on my child's progress?
- What practical experience has the expert in this area?
- Why does he recommend this particular form of treatment?
- Is anyone else offering the same treatment?

Find out how good the expert is

Before talking to an expert, you can find out as much as possible about the kinds of problems you feel your child has by borrowing a book from the library on the subject. If you are thinking of going to a psychologist, borrow a book on child development. Choose ten words that you think have something to do with your worry and look up those subjects in other books. This preliminary research will help you decide whether you really want to proceed and will give you some specific questions to ask.

When talking to the expert, don't be put off by an unexpected answer to one of your questions, but listen to the quality of the answer and the sense of the explanation.

If the expert gives talks or seminars, try to attend one and listen and ask questions. You may find that the expert answers questions in a very understanding and sympathetic way. Even if you are not confident at the way questions are dealt with, you will at least be forearmed if you decide to make an appointment.

Don't let others put pressure on you

Anxious parents sometimes forget all their smart consumer skills. When you are looking for a solution for your child's problems and talking to experts or enrolling in courses, remember that you are the customer as well as the parent. Remember to ask how long the expert thinks that the program will take and why. You may be able to speed up the time if the expert suggests ways you can support his work with your child. Quick fixes do not happen often. They rarely happen without parental involvement.

Parental support and involvement is always helpful so long as you are learning how to help your child and keeping your mind open to all the possibilities for you both.

BEWARE OF:
- experts or people who run courses who minimise your child's strengths and maximise the weaknesses
- experts or people who run courses who say all behaviour can be excused because it is expected from someone with that label

REMEMBER:
All children, except very exceptional children, will have strengths and weaknesses.

WHAT ALTERNATIVES ARE THERE TO LABELS?

It is possible to change children who have school reports saying they can't, into children who can. This applies to all children whenever the problem is one of a lack of understanding or concentration which can be overcome by good teaching. It also applies to children who are labelled ADD.

REMEMBER:
- Problems will be overcome faster when parents and teachers are supportive and want to learn as well.

PARENTS, TEACHERS AND CARERS CAN:
- overcome problems that children have
- teach children how to concentrate and pay attention

When you are looking for a solution to your child's problems and talking to experts or enrolling in courses, remember that you are the customer as well as the parent.

Attention matters

10 QUESTIONS

LEARNING WHEN TO PAY ATTENTION

'AM I TO BLAME FOR MY CHILD'S DIFFICULTIES?'

LEARNING CAN BE FUN

10 QUESTIONS

- Are you paying attention?
- Have you any other thoughts in your mind?
- Are you thinking of the next meal, the child who needs picking up, the report that needs to be written, the colleague who is driving you to distraction, the next load of washing, or the program you want to watch on television tonight?
- Have you read every word in this book so far?
- Do you know where the book was printed?
- Does it matter?
- Have you got ADD?
- Do you know how to pay attention sometimes?
- Are you paying attention now?
- Are you finding it difficult to concentrate reading this?

LEARNING WHEN TO PAY ATTENTION

How much attention we need to pay at any time depends on the particular situation. We only know how much attention we need to pay through experience and we only know where to direct our attention through knowledge and experience.

- Knowledge comes from information or experience.
- Experience comes from practising a combination of skills, while applying what is already known to a new situation.

HAS YOUR CHILD GOT ADD OR:
- does he know how to pay attention sometimes?
- does he only pay attention when it suits him?

When children do not pay attention when they should, they miss out on opportunities to gain experience and knowledge.

When children are paying attention, they gain information, or skills, or a chance to practise. Then they can learn.

Children can be taught to pay attention.

Every child learns differently. Some children will seem to pay attention automatically. However the ability to pay attention doesn't come naturally. The child who pays attention behaves in a way which makes people want to help him more. The child has created a situation where he can be given help.

HE WILL:
- feel confident to continue to use what he knows will work
- feel confident to experiment with new ideas
- realise he can learn a lot
- know how to think about what is around him
- feel successful

**A child who can pay attention
in a particular situation
will be aware but focused.
He will always gather information to help him
play his part.**

A child who can't pay attention has the opposite experience. He will close himself off from the world around him. He will feel he can't be successful. The situation he creates won't make him feel successful.

PEOPLE WILL:
- find it difficult to think of ways to help him
- find it difficult to give him explanations that make him feel he can learn a lot

**A child who cannot pay attention
in a particular situation
may be aware but unfocused.
He will miss important information
and therefore not be able to play his part.**

Being able to pay attention makes a difference.

YOU CAN:
- stay open to the world around you
- remain focused on what needs to be done

- discover the bits you can do
- decide on the order in which they can be done

FEEDING THE HORSES

Karina loved feeding horses. From an early age she was encouraged to think about what she could take out with her, and to feed a horse if she saw one. Karina would find some carrots before setting off with her grandmother. When they got to the field Karina would find a stone and tap on the metal gate. When the horse came she would throw the carrots through the gate for it.

Paul liked feeding horses, too. His grandparents would collect the food, collect Paul and drive to the field. Paul would chat to his grandparents. His chat was random and tiring. He was unaware of the planning that had gone in to getting him to the field where the horses were. Paul's grandparents thought they should give Paul pleasure and his excitement would come as the horse took the carrot.

Karina's grandmother knew that Karina could have just as much excitement and pleasure in planning and preparing to feed the horses, not just at the point where the horse took the food.

'AM I TO BLAME FOR MY CHILD'S DIFFICULTIES?'

Whatever you do don't criticise yourself—you are doing your best

As a parent you take your responsibilities very seriously. You will want to protect your child and will use all your skills to do this. If your child is described as difficult or slow:

- You may be determined to learn how to help your child.
- You may be frightened you won't be able to protect him.
- You may feel vulnerable, and worry that your child's difficulties have been your fault.

Whatever you do don't panic—stay calm

There are many reasons that a child does not pay attention. If you can learn how to stay calm, observant and thoughtful, you will be helping to find the solution to your child's difficulty.

If you can give him time and be at ease as you watch his development, you will continue to devise ways of helping him to be successful, in each new situation he meets.

BEN'S SHOE LACES

When Ben wanted to go to Cub camp he realised he would be expected to tie own shoe laces. His grandad heard Ben's mum say she would explain to the Cub leader that Ben would need help with his shoe laces. Ben's grandad undertook to teach Ben himself before the camp.

He broke the learning down into steps so Ben felt successful at each stage. He didn't give up and although Ben wasn't completely successful by the time the camp came, he was confident of his ability to learn and sensible about getting help for the final stage.

LEARNING CAN BE FUN

If you remember what you were taught successfully by your parents you will realise that you are probably just the expert your child needs. This doesn't mean you cut yourself off from any outside help but it does mean that you can create a child who can be helped.

Your child will know that learning can be fun. Sometimes he will learn everything quickly and sometimes he will need to learn in lots of little steps. Sometimes he will understand something you haven't taught him at all. Other times he will seem to make two steps forward for one step back. That is the delight and excitement of teaching.

PART II
How to teach concentration

DISRUPTIVE BEHAVIOUR

BIZARRE BEHAVIOUR

ALLERGIES

FIDGETING

AVOIDANCE

AGGRESSIVE BEHAVIOUR

TACKLING TANTRUMS AND CHALLENGING
CHALLENGING BEHAVIOUR

NOT LISTENING

DEMANDING

ANGER

WHINGEING

BEING CRUEL

BULLYING

WORRYING BEHAVIOUR

ANTI-SOCIAL BEHAVIOUR

This section is a Do-it-yourself guide to teaching a child to concentrate:

- no matter how outrageous the child's behaviour has seemed to be in the past
- no matter how despairing other people are
- no matter how often you have felt like giving up

I thought I'd be good with kids, but I just can't cope

Your own childhood will have made an enormous impression on you, and will make a difference to the way that you deal with your children.

When you were a child you may have vowed to yourself that you would never treat children the way that adults treated you. But, as an adult, when you find that your skills of communicating with children are not working, you can panic and feel powerless. Because, until you become an adult, you have no idea how difficult dealing with children can be. Realising this can be a real shock.

You may be convinced that you have a lot to offer children. You may be convinced that you know how to get children to respond. To your surprise and alarm, you may find that far from being brilliant with children, you actually find coping with children grim. You may be confused, concerned and constantly confounded by children whom, you were sure, would be respectful, obedient and reasonable.

When children don't respond in the way you thought they would, you might blame them or blame yourself. You might feel you have been let down badly. You might feel you have let yourself down badly. These feelings are not unusual. Don't criticise anyone, especially yourself. You can sort the problem out.

REMEMBER:
- Keep watching and thinking.
- Keep noticing when things go well.
- Keep calm when things go badly.

Remember that a mistake is an opportunity to learn.

Now, you can be good with kids

The chapters in this section describe the specific behaviours which are often used as an indication that a child has ADD. Each chapter concentrates on one particular problem, although we know that every child is a complex mixture.

> **Remember, not only is every child
> a mixture of problems,
> every child is also a mixture of joys.**

Each chapter shows you how to deal with the problems, so you notice (and enjoy) the joys. As you look through this book you may think that we know your child, or you may think your child isn't like any of the children we discuss here. Don't worry, the ideas can be adapted to work for every child.

Each chapter is full of strategies that you can adapt to meet your particular needs or circumstances. If you are feeling that you are a failure, read and re-read the chapters you find helpful. All the chapters have been written to give comfort, advice and confidence to those who have lost their belief in their ability to help children or a particular child.

We recommend that you read and re-read the chapters you find helpful whenever desperation sets in. Every time you re-read one of these chapters, you will see something new.

Flick through the chapters in this section whenever you dread an activity involving your child which reduces you to a sense of powerlessness.

IT COULD BE:
- a meeting with your child's teacher
- an outing with your child
- a visit to grandma
- an appointment with the consultant
- a holiday with friends
- coffee with a neighbour

Lend this book to anyone who has responsibility for your child. You will then have common ground for discussion. It is easier to discuss ideas in a book because the discussion can be focused without being personal. The book operates as a safety net for everyone who is feeling vulnerable. You can dispute the ideas, adapt them or use them as they stand.

Books can help.
Your confidence in your ability to help your child will increase as you use these straightforward ideas. You can help your child and you can help others to help your child, too.

Disruptive behaviour

DON'T PANIC

WHAT CAN YOU DO FOR A CHILD
WHO ISN'T LEARNING?

SETTING THE TABLE

SYMPATHETIC EXPERTS

'I'm at my wits end. It doesn't seem to matter how many times I explain to my child that I want her to be good, she still gets into trouble.'

'I'm sick of my child not paying attention. I feel humiliated when I'm called into the school.'

HAS YOUR CHILD EVER HUMILIATED YOU BY:
- being rude to the teachers?
- refusing to get on with her work?
- disrupting the class?
- being lazy in school?

DON'T PANIC

You can teach your child how learning happens and how to make the most out of her time at school. A child who humiliates you by being badly behaved at school doesn't really understand how to learn or how to let other people learn. Somebody who doesn't understand how to learn, may avoid learning.

A CHILD AVOIDS LEARNING BY:
- wandering around
- sharpening a pencil
- dropping a pencil
- going to the toilet
- asking inappropriate questions
- not having the right equipment
- saying she's got a headache
- saying she feels sick
- not tidying up
- getting something out without permission
- reorganising her bag when she should be working
- losing her glasses
- blowing her nose
- taking longer over the task than is necessary

Your child may think she's got out of something she doesn't want to do. She may think she's justified in getting out of it because what she should have been doing is:

- too difficult
- too boring
- too tedious
- too tricky

WHAT YOU CAN DO FOR A CHILD WHO ISN'T LEARNING

You can teach your child how to learn something at home so she will understand how learning happens. We all learn best if we use what we already know and then think about what else we need to know. You can teach your child to use what she knows. Begin by choosing a task that is simple but does require thought.

SETTING THE TABLE

Setting the table is a good task to start with to teach your child to learn how to learn, because it's an everyday activity which needs a system. Your child will have to keep thinking until the job is finished. You can check when it is finished whether the job has been done properly. You can check whether your child has learnt anything as a result of doing the job properly.

Check why your child wants to get out of it

If, as soon as you ask your child to set the table, she will insist that she is desperate to go to the toilet, don't get annoyed. Think about why she might be wanting to get away. Wanting to get away may be just a habit, or there could be other reasons why she avoids getting on with what she is supposed to do.

- She may think you are unfair. No one else she knows has to do jobs.
- You never ask her brother or sister.
- She may not know what to do.
- She may think she's no good at anything, even setting the table, and has lost her confidence.

Talk to your child about why you want her to set the table. Ask her to tell you why she is avoiding it. Whether she gives you one of the reasons we have listed or tells you another reason, it will help you understand how she is thinking.

How to get started
EXPLAIN THAT:
- she needs to learn how to learn
- you need to help her learn how to learn
- setting the table is the sort of activity that will help you both sort out the problem

Devise a system together
- Find out what she already knows—the number of people eating, which tablecloth to use, the type of meal she is setting the table for, do salt and pepper need to go on the table along with side plates, knives, forks and spoons.
- Tell her what she doesn't know—serving spoons, place mats, mustard, glasses, table mats to put hot dishes on.
- Help her decide which is the best order to get everything on to the table. Try not to tell her the answer.
- Remember, if she makes a mistake it is an opportunity to learn.
- She will find out what she still needs to learn. You will find out what you still need to teach.

MAKE SURE YOU DISCUSS:
- which things are delicate and need special care
- which things will need two hands to make sure they get to the table safely
- which things will need extra care because they are hot
- which things will need extra care because the food is sloppy

Use the system
You can now leave your child to get on with the task, but ask her to call you when she has finished, or be around while she is doing it, if you think you need to, to supervise.

Has the system worked?

Check whether all the things you talked about have been done. If she had trouble remembering for herself, the next time she has to set the table, get her to write a list she can refer to as she goes.

What has she learned and what have you learned?

When you are talking together about what you have both learned, think about whether there are things she has learned that she could use in any other situation. She might have realised that asking for help is all right if she is making an effort herself.

YOUR CHILD MIGHT HAVE LEARNED:

- that asking a few questions before she started would have speeded the whole thing up
- that if she thought about the question first she would have realised she actually knew the answer

WHAT HAVE YOU LEARNED?

You may have learned there are things you need to explain differently.

- You may have learned how to explain them.
- Every child, even one labelled as having ADD, can learn to learn.

HOW IAN LEARNED HOW TO LEARN

Ian was constantly on the move in the classroom. He always had a reason for why he was out of his seat. His teacher thought he couldn't sit still and thought Ian had a very short attention span. She wondered if he had ADD. She realised eventually his real problem was he couldn't do the work she was asking him to do.

When she realised he couldn't do the work she had set ,she taught him the skills he needed. She found he then sat down like everyone else. Ian's problem was solved. He thought he couldn't learn. Now he knew he could. Ian's teacher was a sympathetic expert.

SYMPATHETIC EXPERTS

A sympathetic expert will look at the child. He will notice many of the things the child is doing. He then identifies one thing to be sorted out. The expert will then teach the child to sort out that problem. Some experts teach the parents how to do it. A sympathetic expert believes the child can change and should be taught how to change.

A **simply pathetic expert** on the other hand, just records the child's behaviour and does little to help the child change. A simply pathetic expert believes the child can't change and so has to be protected.

Both sympathetic and simply pathetic experts will tell you your child needs to feel secure and valued. A sympathetic expert will give you reasons why your child is behaving in a particular way. A simply pathetic expert will give you reasons but then use the reasons as excuses for the child's poor behaviour.

Parents and teachers must help a child who is not fulfilling her potential. She needs to overcome the habit of believing she is different and therefore can't learn like other people.

YOUR CHILD MUST NOT:
- fall into the trap of avoiding doing things she doesn't want to do
- believe that difficult behaviour is part of her condition

Experts should show your child how to change her behaviour just as they would with any other child. This should be done with sympathy, noticing how the child is coping and supporting where necessary.

**Check whether the expert
you are consulting
is sympathetic
or simply pathetic.**

Bizarre behaviour

DON'T PANIC

OBSERVATION IS THE KEY

CHILDREN CAN BE TAUGHT HOW TO SPEAK TO OTHERS
WHATEVER THE SITUATION

'I'm sick of my child not paying attention, behaving strangely and making me feel alarmed.'

HAS YOUR CHILD EVER MADE YOU FEEL ALARMED BY:

- refusing to make eye contact
- flapping his hands
- gabbling at strangers
- refusing to let go of a comforter

DON'T PANIC

A child who worries his parents in this way may not realise that other people will think his behaviour is strange. You don't need to be alarmed. You can take each habit that bothers you, explain to your child how it makes other people feel when they see a child behaving in a strange way. They might feel alarmed or they might feel sorry for the child because they think he can't help himself— that he doesn't know what he is doing. Help your child learn how to stop doing it.

Children need to recognise that other people will watch what they are doing and decide whether it is sensible or silly or bizarre behaviour. Children can be taught to think about their own behaviour and think about how they want people to view them.

No matter how alarming, irritating or worrying your child's bizarre behaviour is, nor how lengthy the reports from teachers or experts are, remember what you need to do is watch carefully for an indication that he's thinking, not just reacting to a situation or copying someone else. You may be amazed to discover he can think. If you look you will see him thinking, and when you do, catch the moment because that is the point from which you work with him.

**Children can be taught
to think about
their own behaviour.**

OBSERVATION IS THE KEY

OBSERVING MARK

Mark was four years old and still using a dummy. Everyone thought he had severe communication problems. He couldn't make eye contact and would go into uncontrollable rages if crossed. Mark flapped his hands all the time, especially when agitated.

One day, as Mark's mother described his behaviour to a friend and mentioned his dummy, Mark whispered, 'I use a dummy because I am little.' His mother was stunned when she heard him.

She realised that he was listening and thinking.

She began to talk to him about his age and size and what it meant to be four. She told him four-year-olds didn't need dummies. He took out his dummy and left it on the table. When he began a new activity he put his dummy back in his mouth. To help Mark break the habit of using the dummy, whoever was playing with him would say, 'Pardon?' if he spoke with the dummy in his mouth. Mark began to take the dummy out when he spoke.

By the next day he didn't carry his dummy at all.

His mother was so delighted by his progress she decided to observe Mark when he was flapping. He enjoyed flapping if he was excited and wanting to be busy. Because people thought Mark had a problem they thought flapping was something he always did. Because she was looking more carefully, Mark's mother noticed that he didn't always flap. Mark was tall for his age and had a long body although his arms weren't particularly long. The sleeves of his jumpers, bought to fit his height, often didn't fit his arms and hung down over his hands. When something was over his hands he chose to flap when he was excited. If his hands were free his behaviour was the same as other four year olds—he would smile, laugh, talk excitedly and rush about reporting on what he was doing or what he had seen. He knew how to change an inarticulate flap into showing excitement in an acceptable way using words.

WHAT MARK'S PARENTS LEARNED:
- Mark could operate like a four-year-old.
- Mark could make eye contact.
- Without his dummy and his hands being covered Mark could communicate in a way that was appropriate for his age.
- Mark could progress through the normal stages of growing up.

WHAT MARK LEARNED:
- He didn't need a dummy.
- He could choose to leave babyhood.
- If he spoke without a dummy he could have interesting conversations because people stopped treating him as a baby.
- If his cuffs were turned back he could do more things with his hands like point, stroke, draw, open books and build.
- If he got excited there was lots he could say.

Mark's mother had always thought that his behaviour was a symptom of his problem of communication. She had explained his dummy and his flapping to other people and urged them to be gentle with Mark. Now she was aware that Mark was quite capable of reason and therefore could be taught how to behave. Mark could change his immature behaviour to show everyone, including himself, what he really could do. **He could take responsibility.**

STOPPING TIM GABBLING

Tim couldn't shut up. He was obsessed by dinosaurs. He had no idea how to have a conversation although he was desperate to tell everyone everything he knew about dinosaurs. He had no idea how to talk to people so they could feel involved. He would mutter loudly about dinosaurs but would stare at the floor.

Visiting friends was a nightmare. No one else could hear themselves think, talk to each other or talk to Tim. Wherever Tim went he would take some toy dinosaur and play with it. He would be muttering about his toy and everything else he knew the whole time.

Going shopping was also a nightmare. Tim would glance at a stranger at the checkout and then start talking whether the stranger was listening or not.

Tim's parents decided not to ignore his behaviour any longer. He was now too old for it to be excused. Whenever they went out one of them would be on 'Tim duty'. If he started to gabble he would be taken aside and they would discuss his behaviour with him in a firm but gentle way. He would have to show that he knew why he had been taken aside and say what he was going to do when he rejoined the activity.

SOME QUESTIONS THAT HELPED TIM THINK:

- Why do you think I have brought you away?
- What was the other person doing before you started to talk to her?
- What could you have said first?
- What are you going to do when you go back?
- Were you looking at the person when you spoke to her?
- How do you think you could talk to the person so she would want to talk to you?
- Was it the right time for you to start a conversation with that person?
- What else do you think you can talk about apart from dinosaurs?

Tim learned the art of winning friends and influencing people

Here's how Tim's parents taught Tim to be interested in his fellow human beings so people would be pleased with his interest and want to talk to him.

Tim's parents always made sure, when talking over something they had done with Tim, that they let Tim know why they were pleased with his behaviour. They were careful to mention all the details of his behaviour so that he could think about and remember what he had done that had worked. He would then be able to remember it and practise it again. Here are some examples of what Tim's parents said:

'Wasn't it nice when you smiled and said hello to Jane. She looked so pleased to see you?'

'It was lovely when you joined in the game and concentrated right through to the end. Now you know how to play it we'll be able to play it at home.'

Having a stock of observations or questions which make a social situation easy is a wonderful bonus for anyone—child or adult. A child who notices flowers, an interesting ornament, or that plates need clearing from the table and taking out to the kitchen creates an opening for someone else to reply and be pleasant to him.

**Children can be taught
how to speak to others
whatever the situation.**

Food and allergies

DON'T PANIC

WHAT IS AN ALLERGY?

FOOD FOR THOUGHT

IF YOUR CHILD HAS A FOOD ALLERGY

'I'm sick of my child not paying attention and confusing me. She's so unpredictable.'

'It doesn't seem to matter what I do she just goes off the rails sometimes. I can't understand it and neither can she.'

HAS YOUR CHILD EVER CONFUSED YOU BY:
- being perfect one moment and dreadful the next
- being full of energy one minute and exhausted the next
- being sweet reason one moment and totally unreasonable the next
- learning something easily one day and then seeming to forget it all the next
- being outgoing and chatty one minute and then surly and withdrawn the next

> **If your child has mood swings, think about allergies.**
> **If your child lacks energy, look at the diet.**

DON'T PANIC

Children who have such fluctuations in behaviour may be affected by what they are eating. In consultation with your doctor or dietitian, you can find out what the problem foods are and eliminate them from your child's diet. You can teach your child which foods cause the difficulty and how to avoid them. However, it may be more than one thing that is causing the problem so keep a watch if his behaviour changes again.

> **You can teach your child which foods cause the difficulty and how to avoid them.**

WHAT IS AN ALLERGY

- Some people are affected by chemicals.
- Some people are affected by pollens.
- For some people certain foods can cause problems. Their speech might become slurred and their movements clumsy. They might get angry, depressed or surly.
- Our experience is that children who have a rash, lumps, peeling skin or a perpetual runny nose are taken to doctors who refer them on to a dietitian. Children with poor behaviour may need someone to think about what they have eaten as well.

FOOD FOR THOUGHT

We are all affected by food. Food satisfies our hunger and gives us energy. Sometimes we get more than we bargained for. We get indigestion, feel tense, feel excessively tired or suffer headaches. If we know what causes our discomfort we can stop eating it.

Added to the problems of eating food that may not agree with them, today some children are not eating the right food or getting enough food to give them the energy that they need to grow, do their schoolwork, play with their friends, enjoy life and be pleasant to live with.

Increasingly, some children are hungry throughout the day. Snacking is their only way of eating. They may even feel full after a small snack, but the food they are eating will give them no long-term energy for learning. Many children are irritable because they are always hungry.

If you can get your child to eat porridge or another substantial food like brown bread or rice or pasta, she will have the right food to provide long-lasting energy. Watch out for recipes in books and magazines which will give other suggestions for healthy eating for children and make sure that your child is eating three proper meals a day—breakfast, lunch and dinner.

Here are some useful books that talk about healthy eating for children.

A Healthy Start for Kids—building good eating patterns for life,
  Susan Thompson, Simon & Schuster 1995

Breast, Bottle, Bowl, Anne Hillis and Penny Stone,
  HarperCollins 1993

Busy Body Cookbook, Catherine Saxelby, Hodder and
  Stoughton 1995

Because the behaviour brought on by eating the wrong food or not enough food, or food that the child is allergic to can be so difficult to deal with, an expert, who was just looking at a child's behaviour, could suggest that the child had ADD.

IF YOUR CHILD HAS A FOOD ALLERGY

Much has been written about allergies to food and many people realise that foods with E's, chocolate or orange juice might be a problem. We have worked with children who have gone from co-operative behaviour to defiant behaviour after eating anything that has tomato sauce in it, or whey or bananas. For some children mood swings come about after eating bread, mushrooms or grapes.

You may think your child could be affected by some foods.

* You will already have an idea that there is something odd about your child's behaviour, although you probably won't have linked it with food.
* You recognised all, or some of, the points we have already mentioned.
* Your child swings from being perfect one moment to dreadful the next; from being responsible one moment to destructive the next; from being able to play quietly one moment to tearing around like a banshee the next.

- Nothing you can say gets through to your child.
- You are at your wit's end and your child is out of your control.

You need to remember that your child feels out of control as well, but won't be able to explain to you what is happening. She won't be able to give you reasons for why she has done something awful. She will just stare at you blankly. Eventually the effect of the allergy will wear off, and your child will be free of the awful behaviour.

Some children are very unlucky. Because they are allergic to something they eat all the time, the dreadful behaviour never goes away and people think that the child is horrible. The biggest difficulty with the child who is behaving badly because of an allergy, is that you feel so exasperated with her you don't check whether it is something she has eaten.

It is understandable that adults confronted by the damage, emotional or otherwise, of a child's bad behaviour, will be so upset that a calm look at why the child may be behaving so badly may be impossible at the time. This happens to us and we have had lots of experience dealing with children who behave badly. It is easy to forget to check whether food could be causing the behaviour. What we have trained ourselves to do, is to think about what has gone wrong and if we can't find any explanation that makes sense, we check what the child has eaten.

You, like us, can become detectives tracking down the cause of your child's distress. If your child is always naughty it may help to keep a chart.

**You can become a detective,
and track down the cause of
your child's distress.**

Meals		Sarah's Behaviour			Actions
Time	What Sarah Ate	Time	Good	Bad	
7.30	Toast	7.30–8.00	Got ready for school quickly (Mum)		Had a nice conversation (Mum)
8.00	Orange juice				
8.30				Held up everyone going to work and school	Explained why it was a problem (Dad)

Filling in the chart

You will find that you don't need to use this chart for very long. It will give you the information you need quite quickly.

Melanie's parents were beside themselves. There was never any peace in the house. They described Melanie's terrible behaviour. After using the chart for one day, they picked up some ideas about what the problem might be and they modified her diet.

If your child's behaviour is extreme, keep a record every fifteen minutes and you will probably think of some way of dealing with the behaviour.

Paul's mother was at her wit's end. He'd come in from school like a whirlwind, tipped his juice all over the floor, hit his baby sister and pulled the new electric fire off the wall. She realised that it might have been something that he had eaten and she asked him what he had had. Paul had eaten chips with sauce at lunch time. Now his mum realised why he was being so difficult. She stopped trying to reason with him, and instead took him for a long run in the park. When all the allergic reaction wore off, Paul was his usual self, 'a helpful and happy chappy'.

If your child has an allergy to certain foods, you can teach her to be aware of how she is being affected. You can teach her how to cope if she is getting into trouble. You can teach her how to cope if she forgets things. You can work out ways that she can modify her behaviour as much as possible so she will be safe and so will the other people she is with.

PETER AND THE ORANGES

Peter knew that if he ate an orange he would behave in a violent way and so he was very careful never to accept anything that contained orange flesh or orange juice. One day, just before a football match, he drank some water from a friend's bottle. He didn't realise it had been flavoured with orange. When he noticed he was getting angry he avoided confrontation and played as individually as he could manage.

That was the way he had been taught to cope if he had eaten an orange and was affected by it.

Everybody needs to get to know their body and the reactions they can have at different times.

Many allergic reactions are not going to be life-threatening, but they can affect your child's quality of life—and the quality of life of the people around her.

YOUR CHILD CAN:
- learn to avoid things which cause an allergic reaction
- learn strategies to cope when affected

AND WHEN SHE WAS GOOD, SHE WAS VERY VERY GOOD AND WHEN SHE WAS BAD, SHE WAS HORRID

Anna was a usually delightful child eager to learn and keen to co-operate, but sometimes she became surly, wilful and withdrawn.

For a long time Anna's parents thought it was Anna's character until one day they read about allergies and realised that Anna's mood swings might be related to what she was eating. A friend told them that since she'd stopped eating bread she had felt a lot happier with herself. Anna's parents decided to try leaving out bread from Anna's diet.

The first thing they discovered was that Anna had more energy. They kept Anna off bread, although once when they were visiting relatives Anna had a sandwich. Anna's parents didn't think just one sandwich would matter but almost immediately Anna became difficult. She was surly and rude and when her parents told her off she was worse. She was told to go and sit on her own and she fell asleep. When Anna woke up she was fine. Each time Anna had bread the pattern was repeated. Anna learnt if her behaviour was unpleasant and she had a sleep she would be all right.

Martin's mother was talking to his teacher and both of them were confused by Martin's ability to learn and his inability to remember. They both had many examples of Martin learning something and being able to use it one day, but then acting as if he had never heard anything about the subject at all the next day.

If you have a child like this you need to keep checking and see if the information is used again.

MARTIN'S MEMORY

Martin was excited about his visit to the museum. He told everybody in detail about the exhibits he had enjoyed most. A few days later when he was visiting his aunt his mother suggested he tell his aunt all about it. Martin looked lost and confused. Even with prompting he couldn't think of anything to talk about. It was as though he had never heard of a museum let alone been to one. A few days after that Martin's mum heard him playing a game with his sister where he was a museum guide and she was a visitor. Once again he had lots to say about the things he had seen.

If you become aware that your child does forget things sometimes, but seems to remember them at other times, think about what food she is eating. It may be that what she is eating is having an immediate effect on her memory. Explain to her teacher that she can work normally unless she eats the wrong food. Suggest that the teacher gives your child work to bring home and catch up if she becomes forgetful and starts falling behind.

Children can be taught to remember and be taught to be responsible. Some children take longer than others because something is stopping them learning and until you find out what it is that is stopping them they will continue to have a problem. Food allergies or hunger may not be the problem, but it is worth checking.

**If your child has an allergy
to certain foods,
you can teach her
to be aware of how
she is being affected.**

Fidgeting

DON'T PANIC

WHY A CHILD NEEDS TO BE STILL SOMETIMES

AN ACTIVITY FOR TEACHING A CHILD DIAGNOSED WITH
ADD TO BE STILL

'I'm sick of my child not paying attention and driving me to distraction—he just can't sit still.'

HAS YOUR CHILD EVER DRIVEN YOU AROUND THE BEND BY:

- Jumping around all the time when you're visiting friends and relatives?
- Tearing around madly in the supermarket?
- Always being on the go at home and never giving you any rest?

DON'T PANIC

Children who race around haven't realised there is a still place. Because they don't know there is a still place, they don't realise they can be still. You can teach your child how to go still so he can sit still.

Can you remember when you learned how to sit still? Most of us can remember being asked to sit still, even if we cannot remember learning how to do it. We were given many opportunities to practise sitting still:

- in church
- at the meal table
- on the bus
- in the train
- in the doctor's surgery
- visiting older relatives
- visiting people without children
- playing games

Do you have a child who is driving the teachers mad because he wriggles all the time?

THE CHILD WHO COULDN'T SIT STILL . . .

Samantha always wriggled. She was just five and had started going to school where she would wriggle all through assembly, story time and lunch time. In fact, Samantha was in perpetual motion. The teacher never knew where she was going to pop up next. Samantha's parents dreaded being told, yet again, that Samantha couldn't sit still. Every day when Samantha was collected from school there would be a list of Samantha's irritating behaviour for that day.

'Samantha didn't get on with her work when the rest of the class was busy.'

'Samantha kept interrupting our story time.'

'Samantha was pushing when the class lined up to go into the hall.'

'Samantha is making the teachers on duty at lunch time worry about where she is because she won't stay where they have put her.'

Samantha's parents had always thought that all children wriggled. Gradually Samantha's father began to wonder whether Samantha had a deep problem—different from other children her own age. Her mother disagreed and said lots of the children at playgroup had trouble sitting still. Neither of them could think of what to do. Worse was to come.

Samantha was asked to leave her gymnastics club because she was considered too immature for the teacher to cope. Her constant movement meant that she put herself and others in danger. Samantha's parents were in despair. Other children who had been in the playgroup were welcome at gymnastics.

They decided to see if they could help Samantha sit still. The first step was to watch every aspect of Samantha's behaviour. They found they had set themselves too big a task, so they selected one aspect, her behaviour at mealtimes.

Samantha's parents began watching her from the moment they asked Samantha to set the table until they had all finished eating and cleared away.

THEY NOTICED:
- How many times Samantha had to be asked to do something before she did it.
- How many times Samantha got down from the table.
- How many times Samantha knocked something over because she wasn't paying attention.
- How many times Samantha interrupted someone else's conversation.

When Samantha's parents talked about her behaviour together they realised they had never corrected Samantha's behaviour so she had set her own rules and decided what she would do.

They realised there was a logic behind Samantha's behaviour. Samantha thought that life was a game and was always looking for the fun in it. She hadn't realised that there were many times when she would still be able to enjoy life but she must sit still.

Before going to school she had never been required to sit still. At school, because she never sat still, she never knew what to do next. Samantha thought if you were sitting still you were doing nothing. She didn't realise that when others were sitting still they were hearing what to do next. Samantha never heard what to do next and was never sitting where she was supposed to be.

Samantha found life unfair and confusing. Other people found Samantha irritating and difficult to deal with.

Samantha's confusion led to her behaviour seeming bizarre. To cope with her confusion about what was happening, Samantha would make up her own world. This included telling fantastic stories, as if she believed they were true stories. She made up her own special rules such as 'I must stand up every time the teacher turns a page when she is telling a story'.

All this meant that Samantha was never aware of what was really going on and what other people were involved in, and was unaware of help when it was offered. This is why she didn't keep still when she was told.

It all began to fall into place.

- Samantha didn't know why she had to sit still.
- Samantha hadn't realised she was now part of a group and could learn from the others what to do.
- Samantha thought she knew everything she needed to know and hadn't realised there would be new skills to learn in order to get the most out of school.

What Samantha's parents did to help Samantha sit still

Samantha's mother remembered that when she was at school the teachers taught the children when to sit still. They used signs which meant 'all activity is to stop now and I want you to listen to me'. The children learned what the signs meant.

The reason for the sign was the teacher needed everyone to be still and quiet. This quiet time gave the teacher and the children a break from the activity and a chance to be ready to listen to the next instruction.

The quiet time meant that the teacher was also able to collect her thoughts, speak in a calm voice, take in the whole group as she spoke, and make sure that each child was paying attention.

SIGNS WHICH THE TEACHER USED:

- Standing with her arms folded.
- Standing with her finger on her lips.
- Putting her hands on her head. The children would copy what the teacher was doing and the class would go quiet.

Samantha's mother now understood just why her teacher had used signs. They immediately show children that the teacher wants a pause in the activity. As each child falls quiet and follows the sign, other children notice and quickly pick up what they should be doing, too.

Samantha's mother remembered that at some times of the year or on wet play times when the class didn't fall still quickly, they would have to practise sitting still until they all managed it.

Samantha's parents decided to try some of those methods at home. They were both surprised to find that they were planning to do things their teachers had done with them when they were at school. Previously they thought these must be very outdated methods, but in fact they turned it into a family game—a game of gentleness and delight.

They thought of all the times they dreaded at home. Trying to get out of the house in the morning was the worst. Samantha would make getting dressed a nightmare. She would wander away, put her socks on and take them off again and again, pick up different toys and start playing with them, find herself in front of the television set and never listen. Her parents would be tense, because even though they had tried ignoring the behaviour (a friend had suggested they try this), in the end they knew that they would all be late for school and work yet again.

They decided to teach Samantha a signal which would mean all activity was to stop and she was to listen.

First of all they had to train her to be still. They gave her the choice of which sign she wanted. Once she had decided on sitting with her arms folded, that was the signal for the day. If her mother or father sat with their arms folded, Samantha had to follow suit. If Samantha wanted to catch her parent's attention, she could start the game, too.

Almost overnight the problem of getting dressed in the morning disappeared. Instead of Samantha drifting around the house, she listened when her parents were speaking to her about which clothes she needed. She worked out what order to put her clothes on and listened when her parents made suggestions about what she could do between getting dressed and going out to school. Very quickly she began to take responsibility herself for choosing her own clothes, getting dressed and being ready on time.

Samantha's parents told the teacher what they were doing and the teacher was able to use the same techniques with Samantha at school.

Suddenly other adults who knew Samantha were commenting on how Samantha had changed. People who had never mentioned that they found her difficult began to say how calm she was. People who had never met her before commented on her delightful personality. For the first time in years, Samantha's parents were able to enjoy taking Samantha out, collecting her from school and living with her at home.

Because her parents and teacher cleared up the muddle that Samantha had operated from, it meant that if she did behave strangely, it was easier to isolate the cause.

The teacher noticed that when it came to reading, Samantha's behaviour in class was still unfocused and silly. She then realised that the book Samantha was on was too hard. When she changed the book and Samantha felt successful, her behaviour and her reading improved.

Samantha and her parents learned a great deal about how to help Samantha. Whenever they came across something it appeared Samantha couldn't do, they remembered that they did have the skills to think about the problem and then teach her what she needed to know.

WHY A CHILD NEEDS TO BE STILL SOMETIMES

Teaching children how to be still is fundamental to teaching them how to cope. It will take time and consistency and you will need to take it seriously. If there seems to be a hiccup in the progress, just notice what was different and what new skill you might need to teach. Above all have patience.

Teaching children how to be still will help them at school. By the time a child starts school, even the youngest child will be expected to sit still for at least 5 minutes. This five minutes will increase until by secondary school, the child will be expected to sit still for an hour or more.

AN ACTIVITY FOR TEACHING A CHILD DIAGNOSED WITH ADD TO BE STILL

Can you still be still? The first thing a child needs to know is how to be still. Here is how you can help your child learn to be still.

STEPS TO STILLNESS:
- Ask the child to lie down and see if he can still be still by the time you count to ten—slowly. Lying still means not moving at all.
- When the child moves, tell him which number he managed to get to before he moved and then try again and see if he can get further.
- Take it in turns so sometimes he counts to ten while you lie still. This gives him a chance to see someone else being still.

You can vary the activity—it could be sitting still, standing still or staying still in a funny pose.

These activities will help your child develop and practise self control.

Avoidance

DON'T PANIC

WHAT TO DO ABOUT DITHERERS

HOW TO FIND OUT WHY YOUR CHILD CAN'T DO THE
HOMEWORK

'I'm sick of my child not paying attention and infuriating me by not getting on with anything.'

HAS YOUR CHILD EVER INFURIATED YOU BY:
- always dithering
- always delaying
- never doing any work
- being slap-dash

DON'T PANIC

Teaching your child how to take responsibility for a whole task is an important part of parenting. Your child needs to learn from you how to accept that sometimes something has to be done. You can teach your child how to plan, organise, carry out and complete tasks with the minimum fuss and the maximum benefit. You can teach her to take responsibility.

WHAT TO DO ABOUT DITHERERS

Some children appear to be ditherers—but really they have practised the skill of never doing anything at all. You can recognise ditherers by their tendency always to be 'getting something'. If you ask them what they are doing they are:

- 'getting a pencil'
- 'getting a ruler'
- 'getting a rubber'

And should you catch them more than three times 'getting something', they will say they are, 'getting something for someone else'!

WHY MARCUS DITHERED

Marcus was at a school which prided itself on its academic standards.

When Marcus won a place at the school at eleven his parents had been thrilled. Their delight soon turned to misery because doing the homework became a nightmare.

Previously Marcus' parents had been happy to help him because they realised the importance of homework. Now, they thought, Marcus was old enough to do his homework himself or ask them for help if he needed it. Marcus would sit down and look like he was ready to do his homework. When his parents looked to see what he had done, he'd done almost nothing. Even when they sat with him he did no more. He would look as if he was busy, or about to be busy, but to their consternation, just nothing was put down on paper. If they asked him what he was doing, or made suggestions, he would insist he was coping. If they pressed him further he would cry, shout or storm out of the room.

Marcus' parents knew the school would expect them to make sure the work was done and all homework was done eventually. But it took a stressful three to four hours to get it finished. The homework should have taken about ninety minutes. Marcus' parents had no idea how they could get their family life back on an even keel.

How the real problem came to light

It was just luck that the real cause of the problem came to light. One night Marcus had to look up some information for his homework. There were six or seven books in the house that might have been useful. His parents, when they watched what Marcus was doing, discovered that he had no idea how to identify which books might be helpful. Marcus didn't realise that an index was the best place to start because it would tell him exactly where to find the information in the book. He had always used the contents page and if the exact thing he was looking for wasn't mentioned in the contents he assumed the book was no use. He would pick up books, idly flick through them and then put them down.

It had never occurred to Marcus' parents that this was why Marcus was always having a problem. They thought his flicking showed that he couldn't be bothered. They hadn't realised he did not know. As soon as they understood, they taught him how to use an index in ten minutes. Once Marcus understood how to use an index he began to whiz through his homework. Things he had dithered about before he took in his stride. If he was stuck, he would ask. Family life was a pleasure again.

How the problem happened

From junior school Marcus had been doing projects and had been looking things up. But he had never developed the skills he would need for the kind of homework that would be set at secondary school. He still only had a primary school understanding of how to use a book. He was limited to what it said in the contents. No-one had realised he needed more help. Marcus hadn't realised that his parents would be able to help him out of the muddle. Marcus' parents hadn't realised that he was in a muddle.

It's so easy to blame parents for things they don't know about their children. However it is unrealistic to think that any parent, even the most caring, concerned and vigilant, will always recognise why a problem is happening.

If you are baffled by a child who seems to dither and not achieve anything you can help. We meet and work with many children who are baffled by their homework.

HOW TO FIND OUT WHY A CHILD CAN'T DO THE HOMEWORK

First you need to find out that your child knows what the homework is and understands what is expected.

TO FIND OUT:
* Write down together what the homework is on a piece of paper. Has your child written down what the homework is correctly or may she need to contact someone else to find out exactly what is required?
* Check you both know what is being asked. Remember, a thousand words off the point will get less credit than five hundred words that answer the question.
* Check you both know what is expected.
  Is the answer to be written in essay form?
  How many words is the essay meant to be?
  How much depth does answering the question require?
  Is the question meant to be answered using notes from school?
  Is the student meant to find things out herself?

TO GET STARTED:

- Ask your child to tell you what she already knows and you write it down. Don't panic if she seems to know very little—this is normal. As she tells you what she knows, list the questions about the work that come into your mind
- Look at the list and sort out:

which questions your child can answer without help

which questions need an explanation from you

which questions will need research

what skills does she need to answer the question

what skills hasn't she got that she needs

which skills can you teach her quickly?

THE BOY WHO THOUGHT THE PROBLEM WOULD GO AWAY IF HE SAID 'NO'

Adrian's parents thought they could handle him even though he was quiet and stubborn and delayed joining in family activities. Everyone in Adrian's family kept themselves to themselves and wanted to do things in their own time, so Adrian just seemed to his parents to be a bit more extreme. Although Adrian's behaviour was sometimes inconvenient his parents didn't see it as abnormal.

When Adrian's parents were asked to go to the school to talk about Adrian they had no idea what the teacher's concerns might be. Adrian's class teacher told them that Adrian appeared to be extremely introverted. He would hide under the table and refuse to come out. Even when the head teacher was called to help, Adrian still would not come out. Adrian had put himself beyond the influence of the teachers.

The school policy was that teachers were not to touch children in possible conflict situations unless someone was in danger. There was no way they could get Adrian out without touching him. Adrian had done the same thing at home and with his music teacher when his parents were there. His parents, however, had been able to move him gently to the place they wanted him to be and Adrian had gradually started the activity they had been calling him for.

Suddenly Adrian's parents realised that what had seemed to be a quirk in Adrian's nature that he would grow out of could become a major problem to him. At the meeting it became clear that if Adrian could not respond to instructions like every other child, he could be identified as a child with special behavioural needs. The teacher was constantly having to decide whom to supervise, Adrian or the rest of the class. He presented a danger to himself and to others. It was obvious that if there was a sudden emergency like a fire Adrian would threaten the safety of others. If the teacher simply wanted to take her class to a different part of the school she couldn't leave Adrian.

Adrian's refusal to co-operate on tests for children of his age, meant that his scores were very low. The school felt it had given time for Adrian to develop and mature in the preceding two years but Adrian hadn't been able to catch up with his own age-group and now something would have to be done.

Adrian's parents were shocked to realise that because Adrian had not matured along with his classmates the ball had been put firmly in their court. They were advised that if he had not improved significantly by the end of three months, the school would bring in its own experts. Adrian's parents realised that they needed to find someone who could give them and Adrian some help.

It wasn't easy. Adrian's mother was desperate to find someone who could help. A colleague offered some time, and over a cup of tea they listed all the main things Adrian was refusing to do:

HE WAS REFUSING TO:
- do his homework unless bribed
- go into his gym lessons
- sit at the table in the classroom and get on with his work
- come out from under a table, once he was there

They then identified two things on the list that Adrian's parents could do something about. These were homework and the gym club.

In the past when Adrian had refused to do his homework, his mother had cajoled him for up to an hour before offering him a bribe. If Adrian was interested in the bribe he would do his homework with bad grace. If the bribe didn't interest him then he wouldn't do his homework at all.

The colleague suggested that next time Adrian refused to do his homework, he should be told that he would miss out on television. Adrian loved watching television. Adrian's mother tried this strategy but reported to her colleague that it hadn't worked, because when Adrian had been stopped from watching television, he had gone off and played with his computer.

The colleague explained that, in her opinion, children needed to know that if they did not do what they were told, then they could not make choices for themselves. She suggested that Adrian's mother tell him:

- What time he was going to do his homework.
- Where he would do his homework.
- How long he was going to spend on his homework.

If Adrian wasted any time, that time would be taken off his free time before going to bed and he would be sent to bed that much earlier.

It was important that Adrian should learn that:

- his mother's time was valuable and that there was a consequence for wasting it
- his mother valued the time she spent with him when he tried hard and could spend a lot of time with him then
- his mother would not allow him to waste her time. It was too valuable

When Adrian knew where he would be doing his homework, it was made clear to him that he could not leave that room until the homework was finished or until it was time for him to go to bed—whichever he chose to happen first. This meant that the responsibility was placed firmly in Adrian's hands.

His parents had acted responsibly in telling Adrian what the options were and what the consequences would be. Then they left the decision to Adrian.

Often, Adrian's homework was open ended—learn your two times table or find out about snakes. Adrian had been able to do nothing or the minimum. Adrian's mother now set the standard. Before starting the homework she would say: 'I expect you to look up the dictionary, check an encyclopaedia and make some notes. I will be here to help you, but you will be working all the time.'

After Adrian and his mother had followed this program for a week, Adrian's mother happily reported back to her colleague that Adrian was getting on with his homework without complaint and getting merits from school.

When Adrian's mother went up to school to check how he was getting on, the teacher agreed there was an improvement but pointed out that Adrian was not 'through the woods yet'. The teacher suggested a Home School Book in which she would give Adrian's parents information on how Adrian was getting on at school and where he still needed help.

Here are some comments that Adrian's teacher wrote in the Home School Book.

- 'He hid under the table in the maths lessons and did not come out when called.'
- 'He sat at the table with the other children but refused to do his maths.'

The colleague suggested that Adrian might be afraid of maths and recommended that Adrian do 100 sums a night at a level he found easy. Adrian's mother discovered that any sum which began or ended with a number larger than 9 caused Adrian difficulty. Provided his mother remembered to keep starting at a point where Adrian felt safe, he was happy to work at his maths and became more adventurous with every session. Numbers larger than 9 stopped being a problem.

ADRIAN FOUND THAT:
- Delaying had only been causing him problems.
- He had delayed because he was frightened.
- He could manage his fear.
- Once he wasn't frightened he could manage his behaviour.
- When he managed his fear and his behaviour he could manage to learn.
- Managing his own behaviour brought him success.

Teaching your child how to take responsibility for a whole task is an important part of parenting.

Aggressive behaviour

DON'T PANIC

HOW TO STOP ANTI-SOCIAL BEHAVIOUR

HOW TO HELP A CHILD NEGOTIATE

HELPING AN AGGRESSIVE CHILD LEARN HOW TO PLAY

'I'm sick of my child not paying attention and shocking me.'

HAS YOUR CHILD EVER UPSET YOU BY:
- hitting other children
- snatching
- spitting
- smashing things

DON'T PANIC

You can help your child learn to change aggressive behaviour into behaviour that is acceptable. Your child will be watching other children all the time and he will sometimes try out bad behaviour he has seen and sometimes he will try out good behaviour. If you are worried about bad behaviour don't despair. Make a note of all the times he uses good behaviour then discuss the bad behaviour and explain to him you have seen that he does know the difference. Your child can learn to behave well in all situations and you will be able to help him.

HOW TO STOP ANTI-SOCIAL BEHAVIOUR

Sometimes you can't think what to do. You try everything, but nothing works. It is possible that a friend or relative may be able to help.

STOPPING STEPHANIE SCREECHING

There never seemed to have been a time when Stephanie wasn't a problem. Right from birth she never seemed to be as appealing as other people's children. Other children would smile as they fed the ducks. Stephanie would screech as she chased the ducks. Whenever Stephanie's parents took her out she would spit, throw things and scream. She would constantly run away. Taking her anywhere was a nightmare. She seemed to have no sense of danger.

Her parents were terrified she might drown because she was drawn to water. Her parents were terrified she might get run over because she would go off exploring and often have to be brought back by a worried passer-by. Her parents were terrified she might damage herself because she would climb on anything without seeming to realise she could fall off. Her parents dreaded her starting school—she seemed to be getting more and more out of control.

Every time her parents tried to train her to be safe and obedient Stephanie turned it into a confrontation. Gradually everyone, except her uncle, started to avoid situations which might include Stephanie. Stephanie's uncle recognised in Stephanie something of himself as a child. He had found growing up difficult. He could see the same thing happening to Stephanie. Like many other adults who have had problems as children, he wanted to give his time and understanding to help his niece. He knew that with his support Stephanie could change. He also knew that it wouldn't happen overnight and he must commit time and thought to Stephanie.

The first thing he did was to decide when he could give time to Stephanie. To begin with it was three hours on a Saturday morning. He started by taking Stephanie out. By getting Stephanie out of the house everyone got a break. Stephanie's parents got a break from Stephanie and Stephanie got a break from familiar surroundings where she was used to behaving badly. She also got a break from familiar responses to her bad behaviour. Stephanie's uncle got the chance to see her separately from her usual environment. She was being given the chance to be her own person. If that meant she made mistakes her uncle would have a chance to explain. If it meant she handled a situation well her uncle would have the chance to praise her.

Going out with Stephanie

When Stephanie and her uncle went out, they always walked. Every time Stephanie pulled away, her uncle would hold her still. He would bend down so his face was level with Stephanie's and insist gently that she look at him while he explained the importance of walking together to stay safe. At first Stephanie took any explanation as an excuse for a confrontation. Sometimes when Stephanie behaved very badly, her uncle would take her home and they would start the journey again. Stephanie started to improve but it took many months for her to be able to go out with her uncle without a confrontation of some sort.

When Stephanie's uncle had to miss a Saturday he always went to see her to explain why he couldn't make it. Sometimes he explained why he wouldn't be able to come in advance and sometimes he explained afterwards why he hadn't been able to come. Stephanie's behaviour with other people continued to be erratic. Occasionally it was tolerable but mostly it was dreadful. Even for her uncle she could still behave appallingly. Her uncle however, knew she was capable of more. He did feel terribly disappointed when Stephanie seemed to trash his efforts and his love. She would be walking along beautifully with him and he would tell her how pleased he was and how well she was doing. The next moment Stephanie would pull away even though she knew she shouldn't. She might have seen something which took her attention. If her uncle tried to restrain her Stephanie would scream and the whole relationship that seemed to have been built up would crumble. Stephanie and her uncle would be back to square one.

There were times when Stephanie's uncle felt she would never improve. She would never be able to pay attention, she would never be interested in pleasing anybody and she would always be an unpleasant person to be with. To make matters worse, other people thought he was wasting his time with her.

When he thought about what she had done, he remembered his own difficulties and how he had been helped. He knew if people had given up on him as a child, he would have been stuck and not been able to make the most of opportunities and fulfil his potential.

So that he wouldn't be overwhelmed by disappointment, he kept a list of things he noticed each week. The list included comments Stephanie's parents made about how Stephanie had behaved during the week. In the beginning all the comments were full of despair. Stephanie's behaviour meant that her parents felt they had no option but to give in all the time. Stephanie would hammer the walls, pour milk over the floor and urinate in the garden. Everything Stephanie did her parents saw as evidence of her problems. They didn't feel there was anything they could teach her or anything they could insist on.

When Stephanie's uncle looked back over the lists he realised the comments on Stephanie's behaviour could be analysed and then sorted into different categories. He decided all comments could be divided into two lists:

List 1. Things that had to be stopped immediately.

List 2. Things that were mischief and that any child might do.

Hammering the walls had to stop, but he brought some blocks of wood and nails and Stephanie could use her hammer with those. She loved it.

Spilling milk had to stop. If Stephanie wanted to pour milk she had to do it from a small container which she could control.

If she wanted to urinate in the garden she could do it as long as it didn't cause offence to anyone.

Stephanie was told that often adults would agree if she asked for permission before she wanted to try something. They would be there to help her so she wouldn't get into trouble. He hoped Stephanie would understand because she was about to start school.

It took many months before Stephanie showed she understood how asking for permission worked at school. Her parents were constantly being asked in to see the teacher. Stephanie took time to realise it was not enough to ask permission and then go away and do what she wanted even if permission wasn't given. She had to understand if permission was not given it could be the beginning of a negotiation—it couldn't be a prelude to disobedience.

HOW TO HELP A CHILD LEARN TO NEGOTIATE

It isn't always appropriate for a child to negotiate, but being able to negotiate is an important skill for a child to learn. Here are some negotiating techniques that a child can learn:

- Don't interrupt.
- Use a calm voice—don't whine or bully.
- Give the person you are negotiating with a chance to answer.
- Listen to the reply of the person you are negotiating with.
- Think about the reply.
- If you have another suggestion to make that shows you have listened and thought, suggest it.

Finally, Stephanie began to get an idea of how she could have her wishes taken into account without upsetting everyone else. At about the same time as Stephanie began to understand about asking for permission, her school reports started to improve. Stephanie was able to work alone. She could be trusted in the playground and she began to be good company.

HELPING A CHILD WHO BEHAVES AGGRESSIVELY LEARN HOW TO PLAY

Sometimes parents learn how to cope with difficult behaviour rather than change it. At some point, the child will have to reach a certain standard of behaviour, or risk missing out, being left behind or being thrown out.

KEEPING ELIZABETH OUT OF TROUBLE

'I'm not sure we can keep Elizabeth in our school.'

When Elizabeth's mother read those words she burst into tears. She was angry with the school and Elizabeth. She was protective of her child and understanding but she despaired of her as well. This felt, yet again, like the end of all her hopes.

Elizabeth's mother started to look for another school. She told Elizabeth what she was doing. Elizabeth was upset—she didn't want to leave. Her mother explained that the only way Elizabeth could stay was if she could improve her behaviour and show that other children could be safe around her.

Elizabeth wanted to be friends with people, but she seemed totally unable to tell the difference between a friendly and an aggressive action. Elizabeth always seemed to be hitting other children. When playing in a group Elizabeth might throw a ball nicely or she might kick it with such force it broke a window or hit somebody in the face. Parents of other children were not thrilled to have her anywhere near their own offspring. They didn't want their children to be learning her behaviour and they didn't want their children hurt.

Elizabeth's mother felt people blamed her for Elizabeth's behaviour and she became more and more demoralised. She dreaded being called into the school. She'd always dreaded Elizabeth's grandparents and aunts and uncles making comments about her daughter. She felt that not only were they judging Elizabeth, they were judging her. All the children in her brothers' and sisters' families were boisterous and fun loving but they never went too far. All of them played in a rough and tumble way and were occasionally aggressive or rude, but they could be corrected and never embarrassed their parents in public. But Elizabeth didn't understand she was supposed to stop what she was doing when she was told off. Elizabeth's mother always felt tense when she was visiting her family.

Elizabeth seemed to delight in making every outing a test of nerves. She might walk quietly alongside whoever she was with, or she might suddenly rush off knocking things or people as she went. She was totally unable to cope with meeting anyone she knew in a place where she didn't expect to see them. Her social skills were so limited she would pull a face rather than say hello.

Elizabeth had had fits since birth. Although the fits had stopped, the different drugs she had been given to control her condition affected her behaviour in many ways. As a result her parents had always been completely confused by what they could do to bring her up. For a long time they thought she might have been brain damaged. As a small child she rolled her eyes, she spat and her movements were very jerky and uncontrolled. As she grew older, she seemed unable to respond to any discipline. She would pick her nose and her feet, stab herself with pencils and if she got any small cut she would pick the scab. Her face always appeared twisted and although she was an attractive child she always looked uncared for, undisciplined and unlovely. Her parents felt her behaviour was affected by the drugs. Sometimes they noticed that Elizabeth could be mischievous and delightful, but mostly she didn't understand how far she could go and when she had reached the limit.

Because it looked like Elizabeth was going to be expelled, her mother had a serious talk with her. She explained that even if the drugs had affected Elizabeth's behaviour they would have to find a way of helping Elizabeth behave so people would want her company. Elizabeth seemed to take it in and over the next few days her mother realised Elizabeth wanted to be good. She was making clumsy efforts to be helpful. She was always delighted with any praise. However almost immediately after she had been praised she would do something silly and possibly even self destructive. She would fill her mother and other people, who were trying to help, with despair. It was easy for everyone to forget the good work Elizabeth had done because they felt so let down.

Elizabeth's mother realised that if Elizabeth was going to improve, she had to build on situations where Elizabeth had behaved well. Elizabeth herself needed to understand that she should try to behave well all the time. It was important for her to remember she did know how to behave.

Elizabeth's mother decided to keep Elizabeth under much closer control. She couldn't do it all of the time, but she realised that if Elizabeth was going to feel pleased with her own progress she was going to need very close support. She began by keeping a record on a chart of all Elizabeth's activities and behaviour when she was with her. There was a section for the time between getting up and going to school, a section for the journey to school, a section for meeting her mother and going home, a section for the evening and a section for bed-time. Elizabeth's mother worked and Elizabeth went to after school care. Her mum picked her up at 6.30 pm by which time Elizabeth had had her dinner.

At the end of the first week Elizabeth's mother looked at the chart and realised that although Elizabeth's behaviour had generally been good she had not seen her with other children. Normally at the weekend they would go and visit relatives and Elizabeth would play with her cousins. She was the only girl in the family and she would play for hours with her boy cousins.

Elizabeth's mother wondered whether she should try to see how Elizabeth got on with a mixed group of children Elizabeth didn't know. She took Elizabeth to the park. They took a ball with them and mother and daughter played together. Playing ball with Elizabeth was a nightmare but also a revelation. Elizabeth had no idea how to play with another person. She either kicked the ball straight at her mother or booted it so far in the wrong direction it was a real pain to go and fetch it.

When Elizabeth went to play by the swings she put her face up close to other children and squawked at them. Her mother was horrified.

The next day they went to visit their relatives. Instead of sitting with the adults Elizabeth's mother went out to watch the cousins playing together. Elizabeth's cousins behaved with her in just the same way as Elizabeth had behaved with her mother and the children at the park. It all became clear to Elizabeth's mother. Now she understood that Elizabeth had thought that what she was doing was playing. After all she was only doing what her cousins always did with her. Elizabeth had never understood why her way of playing was so upsetting to everybody because nobody had ever told her cousins to stop when they played like that with her.

Elizabeth's mother began to teach Elizabeth how to play so other people wouldn't be upset. She found a friend with a daughter the same age and invited them round. This gave Elizabeth more opportunities to practise what her mother had taught her. It took time, but it was successful.

Elizabeth's mother told the school what she had discovered and they made opportunities to help Elizabeth when she was playing at school.

One strategy which worked well if Elizabeth was wrecking the game, was to keep the game going, but take Elizabeth to one side. It was explained to Elizabeth that since she was having difficulty coping, her job would be to watch how other people played. Whenever Elizabeth had to watch rather than join in, an adult would explain to Elizabeth why her way of playing wasn't working. Gradually Elizabeth learned to play better. Eventually she could play properly all the time.

Even when a child plays aggressively, the aggression is more likely to happen because there is something the child doesn't know or understand rather than because he has an aggressive personality. If you teach your child the skills needed to cope with the situation where he is aggressive, the aggression will go.

You can help your child learn to change aggressive behaviour into behaviour that is acceptable.

Tackling tantrums and challenging challenging behaviour

DON'T PANIC

TACKLING TANTRUMS

'I'm sick of my child not paying attention, and embarrassing me.'

HAS YOUR CHILD EVER REALLY EMBARRASSED YOU BY:
- having a tantrum when he's out
- saying something rude to you in public
- whingeing and pulling on you when you're trying to talk to somebody
- refusing to come when he's called

DON'T PANIC

A child who embarrasses his parents is one who doesn't realise there are some places where you can do things and some places where you can't. Don't be embarrassed. Every child needs to learn how to behave in public.

HE NEVER DOES WHAT I TELL HIM! HE JUST IGNORES ME

Zak's mother dreaded taking him anywhere. One of the things she hated most was being embarrassed. When she called him he wouldn't come. She couldn't bear the looks other people gave her and him. She was at her wits end. Her confidence was going. She didn't know whether there was something wrong with Zak or something wrong with her.

How the problem disappeared

One day, while Zak and his mum were visiting his aunt, his mum got a chance to see what the problem was. The two sisters had been talking about Zak. His school was finding him too difficult to handle. His mum was crying and her sister was concerned.

Zak had gone off into the garden while the adults were talking. When Zak's aunt called him, because it was time to go home, he ignored her completely. She kept calling his name but he just didn't come. When he eventually turned up Zak's aunt asked him why it had taken so long for him to come. Zak looked puzzled, so she asked him how many times he thought he should be called. Zak thought and then said 'a lot'. His aunt asked him how old he was and Zak said he was seven. She then said 'Well how many times do you think a seven-year-old should be called? Again Zak thought and then said, 'Seven'. Zak's aunt explained that seven-year-old boys should come as soon as they are called—that being seven means you are old enough to take responsibility for getting yourself where you need to be. Zak seemed surprised and fascinated by this information.

It had never occurred to Zak that he was supposed to come immediately he was called. He thought being called was an invitation to come when he was ready—not a requirement to come now.

Like many children Zak took the point straight away. When he was with his aunt he only needed to be called once. He still needed reminding in other situations for a while until he realised that it was a universal rule—when you are called, you answer and come as soon as you can.

What had Zak learned?
* He had learned that when his name was called he should answer.
* He had learned that when his name was called he should come as soon as he could, and not at his own convenience.
* He understood that he was responsible for being where he should be.

What had Zak's mum learned?
* Zak could think.
* Zak could listen.
* Zak was capable of holding a conversation about himself, his behaviour and then change as a result of the conversation.
* Zak could learn to take care of himself.

Zak's aunt was thrilled that at last she had found some way to help her nephew and her sister.

When a child becomes surprised and fascinated by a piece of information the real work begins. It is important that no one thinks the work is over because the child has one insight. Zak still needed reminding in other situations until he learned that he should always do what he was asked wherever he was.

TACKLING TANTRUMS

TONY'S TEMPER TANTRUMS

Tony was the youngest in a family of six. He was determined to get his own way. In order to get his own way he would bully, throw temper tantrums and make it impossible for his mother to talk to anybody if he was with her.

At school he would take no notice of what was going on and just do what he felt like. Sometimes he played and sometimes he lay on the floor and kicked his legs. Often he would talk loudly and interrupt whoever was speaking.

How Tony's family made rules

Everyone gave in to Tony, including his teacher. His mum did it for a quiet life and his teacher did it because she thought there was something wrong with him and was waiting for him to be assessed. Anyone who had to look after Tony became exhausted quickly. If he didn't get his own way, he would keep on until everyone was so worn out they would have to give in.

Nothing changed until the day Tony's dad was collecting Tony's older brother from Cubs. He took Tony with him to give Tony's mum a break. When they got to the church hall, Tony rushed on ahead—straight into the room where the Cubs were meeting. Tony's dad was worried that he might be ruining the meeting. He couldn't believe his eyes when he walked into the hall and saw Tony sitting quietly, listening to the Cub Leader. Tony's father had never seen Tony sit and listen. Usually he would be causing mayhem. He decided, if Tony knew how to behave in one situation, it was time he learned to behave in every situation.

At a family conference it was decided that Tony's bad behaviour had to stop. It was exhausting everybody. From now on Tony could:

- stop having tantrums
- sit still in the car
- stop interrupting
- stop hitting
- let his mother talk to other people
- stop bullying the family

If Tony didn't behave properly he would miss out on:

- television programs he liked
- playing with his favourite toys
- being with the others

By limiting the areas to be sorted out and specifying the penalties if Tony didn't behave properly, the family was able to work together. Tony's temper tantrums disappeared completely in three weeks.

Gradually Tony realised there were other options to temper tantrums. His family continued to support him until he could cope comfortably.

How to show a child there are other options

If a child is throwing a temper tantrum it is important that someone is around to make sure he is not damaging himself or anything else.

Each child has a different tactic in a tantrum. Make sure you stay calm, take a deep breath. If you speak to the child use a normal voice—screaming and shouting will only exhaust you and won't change what is happening. Pleading or bribing is counter productive.

Present the child with ideas about how he could be using his time if he wasn't throwing a tantrum. He could be:

- watching television
- playing with his toys
- out with the rest of his family

You might choose to send the rest of the family on an outing so he knows he's missed out on something other people are enjoying.

**If your child is having a tantrum,
stay calm, take a deep breath
and speak in a normal voice.**

Not listening

DON'T PANIC

HOW YOU CAN HELP YOUR CHILD TO LISTEN

A GAME TO ENCOURAGE LISTENING

10 STEPS TO GET YOUR CHILD TO LISTEN TO YOU

ANOTHER GAME TO ENCOURAGE LISTENING

'I'm sick of my child not paying attention and wearing me out.'

ARE YOU WORN OUT BY YOUR CHILD BECAUSE SHE NEVER LISTENS?

- Does she chatter on endlessly to herself, just loud enough to distract you?
- Does she only want to do what she wants to do?
- Does she get away with not listening?
- Does she think you never mean her?

DON'T PANIC

You will be able to teach your child how to listen so she can communicate sensibly. She can learn why listening is important. She can learn to listen. She can learn to listen to instructions, take part in a conversation and be part of an audience.

HE NEVER DOES WHAT I TELL HIM—HE JUST JABBERS ABOUT SOMETHING ELSE

Scott's parents were convinced Scott could listen but they couldn't get him to. Scott would never look at them. He would keep talking non-stop about some subject that interested him. If his parents tried to take an interest in the subject, Scott would not respond to them. He preferred a monologue to a dialogue. Scott had no friends. His parents thought maybe he had low self esteem. They thought his babbling might be his way of trying to get people interested in him—but it didn't work. Scott's favourite subject was astronomy. His parents bought him books about astronomy. He joined a children's astronomy club which sent him a monthly magazine. His parents encouraged him to write to other children in the club. His parents took him to talks at the museum on astronomy. But, no matter what his parents tried, Scott still babbled and other people gave up talking to him.

How the problem disappeared
One day the whole family visited friends who were on the Internet. It was suggested that Scott could use the Internet to contact

someone who was interested in astronomy. It was explained to Scott that the other person wouldn't know everything in Scott's head. His friend said, in his experience, the best way to sort your ideas out was by writing down all the questions the other person might ask you. You could also write down all the questions you wanted to ask him. Scott would have to communicate clearly. Scott was very enthusiastic.

Scott sat quietly and wrote down all his questions. Once he had finished all his questions the others in the party asked Scott questions to make sure he was thoroughly prepared. Scott used the Internet and was very excited when he realised he could get and give information.

His parents hoped they had found the key.

What Scott learned

- If he had conversations, he could have friends.
- He could have conversations, if he listened and thought.
- If he listened and thought he would be able to give an answer that would make sense.
- An answer that makes sense would give the other person a chance to ask him another question or make a comment on his answer.
- From this Scott learned why listening was important and how dialogue happens and the pleasure of what he was saying being understood and answered.

What Scott's parents learned

- Scott was capable of holding a conversation.
- If Scott reverted to jabbering, they would remind him of how successful he was on the Internet and work with him on how he could make himself understood even when he wasn't on the Internet.

GETTING CLARE TO LISTEN

Clare seemed to be in control even though she never listened. Although she was six, she'd never needed to listen carefully because the five older members of her family listened for her and told her what to do. She was noisy, demanding and selfish. She wouldn't take any notice of anything around her unless it suited her. The family found her amusing and cute but everyone else found her a nightmare because she wouldn't listen.

At school the teachers were finding Clare difficult. They said they thought Clare had a problem actually understanding words. Everyone in Clare's family knew she could understand when it suited her. They had seen it happen at home. They were horrified to realise that Clare's disobedience, which they always found cute, might be interpreted as a learning difficulty. They set aside half an hour a night to teach Clare the importance of:

- listening
- showing people you were listening
- doing what you are told

The whole family discussed how they could help Clare. They realised that everyone would have to stop seeing Clare as a cute doll and instead see Clare as a cute six year old.

How the family changed to help Clare change
THEY STOPPED:
- saying it didn't matter
- laughing at her naughtiness
- teasing her
- getting things for her she could get herself
- defending her bad behaviour
- listening for her

THEY STARTED:
- giving her an explanation when they asked her to do something
- giving her jobs to do around the house
- explaining that listening when someone is speaking to you is good manners
- explaining why good behaviour matters
- insisting that she follow the same rules as the rest of the family.
  If they put their clothes in the washing basket, so would Clare.
  If they took their plates to the kitchen, so would Clare.
  If they didn't interrupt without saying 'excuse me,' nor would Clare.

How the family helped Clare to change

The first thing they insisted on was that Clare should look at the person who was speaking to her. Looking at the person who is talking is important because:

- you show you are directing your attention to what is being said
- the speaker knows she has your attention and so can concentrate on communicating clearly
- you can cut yourself off from what you were doing and focus on what needs your attention now

HOW YOU CAN HELP YOUR CHILD TO LISTEN

1. Choose an activity where you can give instructions.
Clare's family chose putting away the toys before bedtime.
2. Allow enough time.
Clare's family allowed 30 minutes.
3. Get your child's attention.
To make sure they had Clare's attention, whoever gave her the instructions sat in front of Clare, so she was at eye level. If Clare kept talking or kept moving they would hold her shoulders gently, but firmly, and insist that she looked at the person speaking.
4. Make sure your child knows what she's got to do.
Clare's family would tell her what to do and then ask her to repeat back to them what they had said to her. Clare had to keep looking at the person speaking while she repeated the instruction.
5. Make sure your child stays on task.
Once Clare had repeated the instruction she could begin tidying. If Clare stopped tidying before the job was finished she would have to listen to the instruction again and repeat it.

The first time Clare's family did this, the whole 30 minutes was taken up trying to make eye contact.

Don't panic if your child doesn't do what you want her to do straight away. Learning new habits takes time, for both of you. It is quite normal for a child to take time to recognise that you really mean what you say. Persevere because if you get this one right, the rest will come more easily.

HOW TO MAKE SURE YOUR CHILD LISTENS AND THEN GETS THE JOB DONE

Any time an adult asks a child to do something, it is essential that the child understands that requests require some action on the child's part.

On the first night, Clare didn't tidy her toys away in 30 minutes, so the next night the game stopped 45 minutes early. Clare managed to get everything put away.

CLARE DISCOVERED THAT:
* the consequence of not tidying up was that she lost time to play
* the consequence of tidying up quickly and sensibly when she was asked to, was that she gained time to play

If a child refuses to listen to other people, one consequence may be that people will think the reason she doesn't follow instructions is because she can't, rather than she won't. Teaching your child how to listen is important, and anyone can do it.

A GAME TO ENCOURAGE LISTENING

The purpose of the game is to give children an opportunity to practise listening to an instruction and working out how the instruction applies to them.

I'll do one thing while you do another
(This game can be played with one child or a group.)
1. Ask the children to walk around or sit in a group—it doesn't matter which as long as they are ready to listen.
2. Give the children an instruction such as: 'Everyone fold their arms while I put my hands on my head'. The children follow your instruction.
3. Once they've completed the first instruction, the next one could be: 'Everyone fold your arms while John and Tom put their hands on their heads.'

4. Continue giving different instructions and using different children. You might identify the children by what they are wearing, the colour of their hair or the number of letters in their first names such as: 'Everyone with white socks, sit down. People with grey socks, stand on one leg.'

SKILLS THE CHILDREN LEARN ARE:

- how to listen to a long instruction
- how to identify the important points of a sentence which gives information
- how to take part in a game in a group
- how to co-operate even when the focus of attention isn't directed at you
- how to be active and not passive

'DO YOU HEAR WHAT I SAY PHILLIP?'

Phillip never brought a message home from school. His handwriting was so untidy the notes in his homework diary could not be read. Any letter from school would be lost on the way home and any verbal message would be forgotten, if it had ever been heard. Phillip's mother despaired. The situation had been going on for years and she had been told it was Phillip's dyslexia that was the problem but she wasn't sure. She felt Phillip was hiding behind his dyslexia and often just wasn't listening.

How Phillip's mother changed tactics

One day, instead of complaining, Phillip's mother tried a new tactic. She told Phillip that she would teach him how to remember a message. She said: 'Every night we are going to think of things you can write down to tell your dad when he comes in—things he will need to know. I will tell you the information once and you can decide whether you are going to remember it or write it down.'

Needless to say Phillip had not been listening to a word of this, although he had nodded and looked polite. He was surprised when his mother put a pencil and paper in his hand. His mother began, 'Dinner will be at 7.30. Would you like lamb chops or pork chops?' Phillip still couldn't understand what his mother was doing so he put the paper and pencil down. His mother was flabbergasted but undaunted. She said, 'Phillip you are now old enough to listen when something is being said. You are supposed to make a note on that paper. You have to write down what time we are having tea and what the choice of meat is. Make sure you give the message to your father. You didn't bother to listen before, so I hope you are listening now—dinner is going to be at 7.30, would you like pork chops or lamb chops?'

Phillip still hadn't realised that he was supposed to be listening to a whole message and making a decision. He asked if it would be all right if he went out to play with his mates. His mum said he could. At 7.30 when Phillip smelled food, he ambled in expecting to eat. His mother and father were eating but he could see no sign of food for him. He sat down and his mum asked why he was sitting down. Phillip said he'd come in for his meal to which his mother said, 'But I asked you what you wanted and you didn't reply.'

Phillip's parents explained to him that his habit of not bothering to listen had to be overcome and every day they would think of some other way of trying to help him to listen. They would know when they had been successful because they would be getting messages from school through him and he would also be taking more responsibility about listening at home. They would also be giving him dictation practice every night. That way he could improve his note taking so he could read what he had written down in his homework diary. If the reason he was not doing what he needed to do was because he didn't have the skills they would help him to get them.

His mother was amazed that she had gone to the lengths she had of not making him tea. However she realised that Phillip was never going to listen to words unless he could see that listening was going to be to his advantage. People had always compensated for Phillip. Now it was time for Phillip to learn how to fill in his own gaps.

10 STEPS TO GET YOUR CHILD TO LISTEN TO YOU

1. Choose a time when you will not be interrupted—you need at least 30 minutes.
2. Identify, in your own mind, something you want your child to do.
   Putting her own shoes and socks on.
   Putting her clothes away.
   Tidying up an activity when she has finished playing.
   Going to the bathroom to wash.
3. Have your child standing in front of you making eye contact while you explain what you want her to do.
4. Keep the instruction short.
5. If she stops looking at you insist that she makes eye contact again—repeat the instructions.
6. If she doesn't obey you, explain the consequences. Such as, until she has done the task she won't be able to do anything else or if she takes too long she will miss out on something else.
7. When she has finished the task, go over with her what happened.
8. Point out where you were pleased and what you will help her with next.
9. Make your next plan so that the improvement continues.
10. Always remember—eye contact is the key.

Knowing that you should look at the person speaking to you is essential to knowing how to learn.

- Looking at the person speaking means you give yourself the chance to learn.
- Knowing how to look at the person speaking is an important social skill.
- Being a receptive audience will make you good company.
- Knowing you will get most benefit if you look at the person speaking, while you are listening, is an important life skill.
- Looking and listening to the person who is speaking means you get the best chance of understanding what has been said and how you can use what you have heard.

ANOTHER GAME TO ENCOURAGE LISTENING

This is a hilarious game and makes learning to listen to instructions fun. A good exercise is to take it in turns to give each other strings of instructions which have to be followed. The only purpose of the game is to remember what you have been told.

Can you remember?

1. You give your child an instruction such as, 'Build a tower with a blue brick at the bottom, a red brick in the middle and a green brick at the top and come and tell me when you have finished.'
2. After she has finished building the tower, it is your child's turn. She can choose what she wants you to remember and do. She might say for example, 'Pick up the newspaper, carry it to the kitchen and put it in the refrigerator and come and tell me when you have finished.'

**Teaching your child how to listen
is important, and anyone can do it.**

Demanding

DON'T PANIC

HOW YOU CAN ACCENTUATE THE REAL POSITIVES TO
ELIMINATE THE NEGATIVES

HOW TO COPE WHEN YOUR CHILD RUNS WILDLY
AROUND IN SOMEONE'S HOUSE

HOW TO COPE WHEN YOUR CHILD WRECKS THE GAME

YOU CAN TEACH YOUR CHILD TO PLAY THE GAME

TURN TAKING

BODY MANAGEMENT

SUCCESS AND FAILURE

WATCHING

RULES

'I'm sick of my child not paying attention, and being impossible to live with.

HAS YOUR CHILD EVER MADE HOME LIFE DIFFICULT BY:
- demanding your time, your money and sometimes it even feels like your life
- hating his brothers and sisters
- running riot
- getting frustrated easily
- wrecking games others are playing
- thinking it's funny when what he is doing spoils the game for others

DON'T PANIC

It is sometimes hard for children to realise that they affect the group they are with. This includes their family. You can teach your children how to be helpful members of any group they are in.

How to cope when your child demands your time, your money and sometimes it feels like your whole life

ROBERT: THE BLUEBOTTLE FLY

Robert at home was a constant irritation to his parents and his sister. No matter how hard they tried to encourage him to take notice of other people's feelings, he just charged around as though the only person who mattered was himself. He would butt in to conversations, flail his arms and legs about and barge from one place to another. Robert was like a bluebottle in human form.

Robert's parents hoped that Robert's behaviour was more controlled at school. When they were worried and discussed his behaviour at home, they comforted themselves with the knowledge that nobody from the school had complained so Robert must be getting on all right.

How Robert's parents did something about it
They were horrified when they went to parents' night. They thought they would just be looking at Robert's work. Instead they were taken aside and told Robert was so difficult in the school that

outside professional help was being considered. After the shock, they decided that they could do something themselves about Robert's behaviour. They asked the school to keep a daily Home/ School Record Book. In this book Robert's parents wrote down what he did at home and the school wrote down what he did when he was there. After experimenting Robert's parents and the school arrived at a successful format for the book. This format allowed everybody to keep drawing attention to the many positive aspects in Robert's life, at home and at school.

Make sure everyone knows what is going on

There was one setback when a temporary teacher took the class and assumed that the book was a record of Robert's misdemeanours. The policy for Robert's record book was to record Robert's poor behaviour *only* when it was unsatisfactory compared with everybody else in the class. If the whole class came in very noisily after playtime, but Robert was no worse than anyone else, then there would be no record because it was a class matter.

The temporary teacher thought the school wanted her to focus on Robert's bad behaviour. Because it is easier to see poor behaviour than recognise good behaviour this was all she recorded. The effect of recording Robert's behaviour as though everything was bad behaviour was temporarily catastrophic. He felt totally confused because he had no idea why things had suddenly become so dreadful. It had to be explained to him that he hadn't changed but something else had changed. It was a change in the procedure being used, not a change in Robert. Robert's parents contacted the school and the problem was sorted out. The temporary teacher was delighted to be involved in supporting the work with Robert.

HOW TO ACCENTUATE THE POSITIVES TO ELIMINATE THE NEGATIVES

Here is how you can accentuate the positives to eliminate the negatives without deluding yourself and others.

The format which follows on page 106 worked for Robert.

Date:

For a young child use a picture to show when you are pleased	and use another to show when you are not pleased
POSITIVE	NEGATIVE

Robert worked well with Phillip in the library.	When the class went out at breaktime Robert was calling people silly names and upsetting them.
Robert listened beautifully to the music lesson which was in the hall and came up with lots of good ideas for making percussion instruments.	Robert slammed the door because he thought it was funny.
Robert finished his maths sheet and his work was neat. He is trying very hard with his presentation and the effort is paying off.	

10 REASONS WHY THIS FORMAT WORKED

This format worked well for a number of reasons.

1. People now could concentrate on Robert's strengths and isolate his weaknesses.
2. People realised he could be helped to overcome his weaknesses.
3. The report created a visual impact. Seeing so much successful behaviour at school encouraged everybody.
4. The report helped Robert know what he could do to please people.

5. Suddenly what had seemed to be a severe problem became manageable.

6. Robert could see when his behaviour was a problem and when it wasn't.

7. Robert now knew the areas he needed to work on. In the past he was rarely complimented but often criticised because his behaviour was so difficult but he didn't know how to improve. Now it was easy for people to explain when his behaviour was trying. Robert was able to cope with one thing at a time.

8. Irritating behaviour in the past had obscured his good behaviour. There was now a record of behaviour which could be used in different ways when people needed to think about how Robert had got on.

9. The people responsible for Robert at school, in the class or in the playground had a chance to write down what they felt when they were irritated. If they were especially pleased they could make a comment.

10. If there was no comment, then Robert was managing to cope at school like everyone else.

HOW TO COPE WHEN YOUR CHILD RUNS AROUND WILDLY IN SOMEONE'S HOUSE

'Has your child ever run riot and embarrassed you when you have been out?'

LIKE BULLS IN A CHINA SHOP!

Yvonne invited a new neighbour to pop in for a cup of tea. She expected the neighbour's children would behave like her own children when they were out visiting. Her own children would sit still when asked, and be quiet when asked. They would also move around another person's house with care. Yvonne was confused when her neighbour's children charged around her house breaking things without care. The neighbour had no embarrassment or sense that she should be imposing some control on her children.

PARENTS CAN HELP CHILDREN BEHAVE WELL BY:

- taking a game, pencils and paper etc. when they go to visit so children can be given something to do
- explaining to children the behaviour which will be expected

When you take your child out to visit, let him know that if he misbehaves, the visit will end. You will both go home and he can help you with some chores around the house. It is important he doesn't feel he has won when he misbehaves. Explain to him that, if you can arrange for someone to look after him, you will go and see your friend and have the visit that was planned at another time.

HOW TO COPE WHEN YOUR CHILD WRECKS THE GAME

Even adults can find some games difficult to endure. There are many reasons for this.

- You might have been forced to play a particular game when you were young, and remember hating every minute of it.
- You might get caught having to play a game you hate, simply to make up the numbers.
- You might feel you have to join in something everyone else is brilliant at playing, but you have never played it before.
- You might know a different set of rules for the game being played.
- You may be very competitive, and can't see any point in playing the game unless you can win!
- You may be non-competitive, and can't see why people get so worked up about what is supposed to be just a game.
- you may remember feeling a failure.

What is a nightmare for one person can be a game for another.

Children wreck games for many reasons.

1. Children may not be old enough to play them.

Jay's dad was convinced he could teach his son how to play chess. He felt anyone who could play chess would have a great advantage in life. Jay was too young to grasp the rules quickly enough for his dad and his dad became impatient. Jay tried to please his dad but he hated chess and knew if he kept going to the toilet his dad would get fed up and the game would end.

2. Children may not understand the strategies or the techniques needed to make the game enjoyable.

Rebecca hated jigsaws. She couldn't see any point in doing them and had no idea how to get all the pieces to fit together anyway. Even when people showed her strategies which would work she couldn't take the information in.

3. Children are acting out behaviour they have seen their heroes do.

Robbie wanted to be a footballer. He practised everything his footballing hero did. He practised free kicks, tackling and shooting. His hero was one of the 'hard men' of football, so Robbie practised intimidating the opposition. No-one wanted to play football with Robbie.

4. Children may not know how to focus on an activity.

Eleanor always wanted to play games, but never knew when it was her turn. If she was playing a game inside the house she would drive everyone to distraction because she would slow down the pace of the game until it became unbearable. If she was playing basketball, rounders or any other team game, she was never looking. The rest of her team found her irritating. She was always last to be picked.

5. Children may feel they always have to win.

Tim would keep changing the rules all through the game, until it was impossible for anyone else to win. If he was playing with a bigger person, he would demand that the bigger person give him plenty of chances. If he was playing with a smaller person he used his size to gain advantage.

6. Children can't set themselves up for failure.

Rashid loved dominoes. He was always fascinated when he began the game but if he realised he was going to lose he wouldn't make a fuss about losing, but would just wander off or suggest another game.

7. Children want their own way and will bully to get it.

Zoe nagged all the time when she was playing a game. No-one would play with her unless there was an umpire who would control her behaviour. She would become angry with each competitor in turn intimidating everybody.

YOU CAN TEACH YOUR CHILD TO PLAY THE GAME

Games can be fun or fearful; they can be fascinating or frustrating; they can fuel friendships or feuds; they can create harmony or hate. The way to make sure game playing is pleasurable is to teach your child the skills involved in being a pleasant participant.

An A-Z of Skills for Games

Attention	Noticing what's happening
Being ready	Observation
Coping with losing	Planning
Decision making	Quick responses
Enjoying another's success	Remembering the rules
Following the rules	Sharing
Getting ready	Thinking
Having patience	Understanding the rules
Intelligent action	Valuing other players
Joining in	Watching others
Keeping still	eXercise
Looking	Your turn!
Managing your body	Zing!

TURN TAKING

You can help your child become a successful game player by teaching him how to take turns.

Peter was always allowed to be first in the games at home because he was the youngest. He didn't understand that when he played games away from home he wouldn't always be first. He found games difficult when he wasn't playing them at home and felt confused and unhappy.

Teach your child to take turns wherever he is—don't always let him go first, win, take too long over his turn.

Stop the game if he is being nasty, impatient or cross. Explain why you have stopped the game and be quite firm about what you expect before you start the game again.

Involve him in making a list of things he can work on to learn how to take turns nicely. You might concentrate on one thing at a time so he really understands what you are trying to teach him.

BODY MANAGEMENT

If all players control their bodies when playing a game—from dominoes to basketball—the chances of the game being wrecked are reduced dramatically.

Learning how to control your body, involves finding an appropriate way to sit, stand, run and stop. Any board game needs players who can be careful not to knock the pieces. Any ball game needs players who can be careful not to knock other players. When children are outside playing encourage them to:

- keep their eye on the game even when they haven't got a bat or a ball in their hands
- run without knocking into anybody else
- notice boundaries such as flower beds or the road
- notice other people who might be using the space but are not playing the game

Some children are poor at controlling their movements, but games which involve them responding to instructions will help them.

A GAME TO HELP GIVE CHILDREN BODY CONTROL

In this game, you give your child instructions that will give him skills and help him with body control. Here are some suggestions.

- Run forward.
- Stop.
- Run backwards.
- Stop.
- Gallop sideways.
- Stop.
- Run on tip toes.
- Stop.
- Run in a circle.
- Stop.
- Hop.
- Stop.

Use any other instructions you think would add to your child's skills. You can add instructions like the number of steps. Then go on to link instructions together so your child follows one exercise with another.

- Run forward fifteen steps
- Run backwards five steps and then run in a circle.

SUCCESS AND FAILURE

You can teach your child how to be happy about playing games, whether he is winning or losing, if you talk to him about why games are played. Here are some reasons.

- To develop skills.
- As a form of entertainment.
- To notice your own progress.
- To develop thinking.
- As a social event.
- As a way of using up energy.
- For something to do when there's nothing to do.

A game can include specific rules, which are only applied when that game is played, such as you go up the ladders and down the snakes. General rules apply all the time, such as sharing, not snatching, being supportive of others.

If a child has spent a lot of time playing computer games, where he has competed against the computer, he may not realise, when playing with other children, that they have feelings.

If a child has only played games against adults who have not taught him how to play equally, he will find playing with children of his own age very difficult. He may think people don't like him, when what they really dislike is the way he is playing. Both sets of children are missing the experience of learning how to give and take. They will be frustrated and make others feel frustrated too when they make unreasonable demands. They always assume their needs are paramount and should be met.

Graham loved playing a memory game where players had to turn over pairs of cards to try to find matching pairs. He was good at the game and would tell all the other players which cards to pick up. If they picked up the wrong cards, he would berate them. He saw the game as only existing for himself and the other players as keys to be pressed. Graham had no idea that the other players were hoping to enjoy the game using their skills and were not just pawns in his game.

WATCHING

When you're playing a game you alternate between being an audience or a participant. In both roles you need to be active—watching, thinking, planning or moving. You need to be paying attention to the changing circumstances as the game progresses. You need to be planning what you can do next and what you will do if another player blocks your move. You need to get the pacing right and enjoy playing with the people you are with and not nag them because they are faster or slower than you. If you can watch carefully, you can enjoy the whole game and avoid the frustration of having your planned move blocked, because you will enjoy seeing how the other person is thinking.

Rules

Rules are a shorthand way of negotiating your way through what could be a difficult situation. Your child can become a good game player, if you help him to understand that he needs to pay attention to the rules because they matter. He needs to know that when rules are being explained it's important to listen. Your child also needs to know that a game he enjoys can still be fun even if he's playing with someone who uses slightly different rules for the same game.

Sadia was lonely because she had no friends. Here's how her mother helped her.

TEACHING SADIA HOW TO PLAY WITH FRIENDS

Sadia's mother suggested a game to Sadia. They would both play at having a friend round for the afternoon. Sadia's mother would start—Sadia would be her friend and she would come round to play. For a few hours Sadia's mother played the role of a sensible and caring child who was entertaining her friend. Sadia was so fascinated by the idea of her mother pretending to be a child she played happily with her for the afternoon. All the time Sadia was seeing how it could be done.

The next afternoon the roles were changed. Now it was Sadia who was entertaining her friend. They decided to play ball. Whenever Sadia did something silly with the ball, so it spoiled the game, her mother would explain the effect that would have on the game and on the people playing it with her.

Sadia's mother took two roles on this afternoon—the friend and the supporter. As the friend she would play happily. If something went wrong, she would take the supporting role and explain what had happened, what the immediate effect of that was and what the consequence of that might be. They then talked about what Sadia could immediately do to make things better.

Only when Sadia felt successful because she had made amends, did her mum talk about how the situation could have been avoided in the first place. Then they went back to playing again.

Sadia's mother was being a sympathetic supporter, not a simply pathetic defender.

Anger

DON'T PANIC

HOW TO TEACH YOUR CHILD TO COPE WHEN YOU MEET

WHY CHILDREN CAN BECOME ANGRY

DON'T FORGET TO WRITE A LIST

WHY CHILDREN 'LIE'

HOW TO COPE WHEN YOUR CHILD TELLS YOU A 'REAL'
STORY

'I'm sick of my child not paying attention, and frightening me.'

HAS YOUR CHILD EVER FRIGHTENED YOU BY:
- lying
- playing dangerously
- just not knowing why he is in trouble
- being fascinated by animals but unacceptably rough
- getting angry when anything upsets him
- never doing what he's told

DON'T PANIC

If you have a child that needs to be taught how to behave, stay calm, there are ways of teaching her. Some children seem to know how to behave in every situation. Most children need to be taught.

THE BOY WHO BROKE THINGS

Dominic was always shouting and breaking things in anger. This seemed very strange, because when Dominic wasn't angry he was really a helpful and accommodating person.

Dominic's dad had shouted and broken things most of Dominic's life. Eventually, Dominic's dad found another way of dealing with his frustration. He stopped breaking things and shouting. Instead he went into his room until he calmed down. Because he didn't tell Dominic what he was now doing, when he was stressed, Dominic continued to shout and break things because that's what he thought people did when they were upset.

One day, after an argument, Dominic asked his dad why he had gone off into his room. His dad told him he went to his room when he felt angry, and when he had calmed down, he would come out again.

Dominic then used his own room as a bolt hole when he noticed he was stressed. The shouting and breaking things stopped.

What Dominic learned
- We are all affected by other people.
- We may measure ourselves against other people.

- As we grow up we realise copying *some* people will benefit us.
- As we grow up we realise copying *some* people may be a waste of time.
- As we grow up we realise copying *some* people may be harmful.
- Some people we are copying may have changed, but we are stuck copying something they have decided doesn't work.

THE GIRL WHO WAS NOISY ALL THE TIME

Sally loved the Power Rangers. They gave her the freedom to be the way she wanted to be.

Sally had a severe hearing problem and felt devalued by everyone. She appeared to be a slow learner because what she heard was so muddled. She found acting as if she was one of the Power Rangers a great relief. Her parents and teachers didn't realise what she was doing and thought she had severe behaviour problems. Once they did realise, they were able to tell Sally how much they admired her. They told her how brave they felt she was, and how much determination they had seen her show when she kept on working, even though hearing was so difficult. They explained there was nothing wrong with pretending to be a Power Ranger as long as you kept safe and weren't doing it when it interrupted someone else. Sally understood, and from then on her behaviour in the classroom improved and she confined her Power Rangers play to the playground.

What Sally learned

- She was admired for her own qualities.
- There was a time when she could experiment with new ways of behaving.
- If she experimented at the right time it wouldn't upset anyone.
- There is a time and a place for everything.

THE BOY WHO 'WENT OFF THE RAILS'

Adam had always worked hard and everybody liked to teach him. His parents started to get different reports from teachers when Adam had been in secondary school for two terms. For the first time Adam was being described as rude and disobedient. They knew Adam might have problems, like any other child, going from a small primary school to a larger school where all the requirements would be different. They had comforted themselves with the thought that he was good academically, hard working and polite. In the first term there had been an isolated incident of bullying but it had been resolved.

When Adam's parents talked to him, they asked him who were his friends in the class. They suggested he invite his friends home for tea. Adam had three friends and when they all visited they were no trouble at all. They chatted and laughed and seemed similar to Adam.

Still the teachers complained about Adam's behaviour. He was getting detentions and being kept behind. Adam thought it was all very unfair. His parents rang the school and arranged to meet with one teacher who was always giving him detentions.

The teacher explained that when Adam was in his class he was always messing about and not doing what he had been asked. The teacher said there were four boys who were a constant problem. They were the boys who had come home for tea.

How Adam's parents solved the problem

Adam's parents sat down with Adam and explained what teachers needed from their pupils.

- Co-operation.
- Quiet.
- Work.
- Politeness.

They asked Adam which ones he thought he was doing. Adam began to cry. He said if he was good he would be bullied. If he did the same as the other children who were getting into trouble he would be safe from the bullies.

Adam's parents explained that all his life he would come across people who might try to bully him and now was the perfect opportunity to learn how to cope. They asked him if anyone else in the class was a hard worker and whether that person was getting bullied. Adam said there was one boy and all the rest were girls and as far as he knew, horrible things were said about all of them because they were hard workers.

Adam's parents pointed out that even though these children were being bullied they weren't choosing to misbehave to protect themselves. They wrote down the choices Adam could make.

- To continue as he was.
- To sit near the people who were working.
- To ignore his three friends altogether.
- To play with his friends in the playground but be separate from them in the classroom.

Adam found a way to cope and the teachers' complaints stopped.

What Adam learned
- That he could make choices about his behaviour and could stop getting into trouble.
- You could still have friends and yet not be influenced by the same people when they were behaving badly.
- He had a responsibility as a pupil to make sure he didn't stop the teacher teaching.

THE GIRL WHO WAS NASTY TO HER MUM

Natalie's mum was thrilled the day Natalie started school full-time. She and Natalie had eaten a special breakfast, the sun was shining and Natalie looked neat and tidy for once. They walked to school together chatting happily about what Natalie might do that day.

As they got close to the school, Natalie's mum hoped that Natalie would enjoy her first day. They saw an older child stomping ahead of her mother, ignoring her mother's good-byes and marching into school. As Natalie and her mum parted Natalie's mum said, 'You'll be able to tell me all about it tonight.' Natalie's mum stayed brave while she waved Natalie goodbye. She was overwhelmed by emotions as she walked away from the school.

At 3.15 pm she was already at the school waiting for Natalie to come out at 3.30. Natalie's mum smiled as Natalie came out of the school. But the smile froze on her face as Natalie walked towards her. She had never ever seen Natalie looking so resentful and bad tempered before. She stepped towards Natalie to give her a hug but Natalie just grunted, shoved her bag at her mum, pushed past her and set off walking home.

How Natalie's mum solved the problem

Natalie's mum was dumbfounded, then she was hurt, then she was cross and then she was determined. She caught up with Natalie and walked alongside her. She tried to think where this extraordinary behaviour might have come from.

It took her some time to realise that it was probably what Natalie had seen as she walked into school. She was 'trying out' being an older girl. Her mum explained that there were other ways to behave if you wanted to be seen as a big girl and the next day they would get to the school early and watch the different ways of saying goodbye.

Natalie's mother was fortunate to see where Natalie's hurtful behaviour came from. If your child is doing something you don't like, explain that there are other ways of behaving. Then go and watch a group of children dealing with similar situations in different ways.

What Natalie learned

- Never knock your friends (or your mum).
- New experiences need new learning.
- You can make a mistake and learn from it.
- You need to look carefully to see which sort of person you want to copy.
- If you make the wrong choice you can change it.

HOW TO TEACH YOUR CHILD TO COPE WHEN YOU MEET

Sometimes you need to prompt your children into the sort of responses that are possible. When meeting them out of school encourage them to tell you what they have been doing. This will get rid of (or reduce) the demand for a treat. All children need to learn how to suit their conversation and behaviour to the situation. If they don't learn it, they can get stuck in something which is totally unhelpful to everybody. After school, take the opportunity to tell your child about your day as you are hearing about hers. Then plan together what is going to happen next.

THE GIRL WHO SUDDENLY CHANGED

Katy's dad was working away from home. Suddenly Katy had started to speak loudly, order everyone around and get angry whenever she thought something was going wrong. She was unbearable. She wouldn't go to bed on time. She followed her mum around and she stopped playing with her little brother and sister. She stopped doing her homework and would prowl from one room to another. Every so often she would weep hysterically with anger and frustration.

How Katy's problem was solved

First people put it down to the problem of adjusting to her dad being absent. They thought Katy would settle down once she got used to things. They were surprised when they realised the behaviour was continuing. The problem was that Katy thought she had to make up for her dad. She had to take on his attitudes and his behaviour. She thought she should be able to cope with everything as he did. The tears came when she felt she was failing.

Her mum explained to her that although she needed Katy's support, she didn't need her to try and be an adult. They made a list together of all the things Katy had done before her dad's job had changed. They worked out a new list. On this list were the things that Katy would do, her mum would do, her brother and sister would do and her dad would do when he came back. Katy's mum could feel Katy relaxing.

What Katy learned

- Because she was a child, she did not have to take on adult's responsibilities.
- She could help her mum by doing her homework well.
- If you take on more than you can handle, you become miserable.
- When you get confused, a list can help.

WHY CHILDREN CAN BECOME ANGRY

Many children have no idea that learning involves their taking a risk, making mistakes, committing themselves, accepting correction and practising. They think that any time they do anything at school or at home, people expect them to do it quickly, accurately and perfectly first time. If your child is like this she may be aggressive, rude or irresponsible when asked to do anything because she is afraid of failing.

If you explain to your child how you learn something, she will understand that learning is a lot of little steps which suddenly come together to make one big stride. Remind your child of something she has learned successfully, and write down in a list the stages she had to complete before she could do it properly.

DON'T FORGET TO WRITE A LIST

Writing lists means you have something to look back at. Without a list, a conversation which had been important to one person might be completely forgotten by everyone else.

Lists help children become more responsible for their actions.

Remember if your child flies off the handle, check whether she is modelling on someone else.

1. Is she behaving like someone you know—her sister, the girl next door?
2. Does she have a hero or heroine—television character, computer character, book character?
3. Is there a naughty child in her class?
4. Has she heard someone else, or seen someone else do something, and wants to see what will happen when she tries it?
5. Has there been a traumatic change—divorce, death, illness, move?

WHY CHILDREN 'LIE'

Children often reorganise information to get the 'best fit'. They don't really see this as lying and often they will get away with it because there will be no reason for anyone to know that they are not telling the truth.

Sometimes what appears to be lying, is a child's attempt to cope with her emotional needs in different situations. She is too immature to be able to select accurately which pieces of information must be included or excluded for her accounts to be reliable.

HOW TO COPE WHEN YOUR CHILD TELLS YOU A 'REAL' STORY

THE BOY WHO CHANGED THE TALE

John's mum rang John's headteacher to find out what had really been said to John in the headteacher's office. The headteacher explained that John had been told he would be excluded from school if he couldn't do what he was told. He had to get on with his work, be polite to teachers and play safely with the other children.

John's mother thanked the headteacher and said the reason she'd rung was that sometimes John left out important pieces of information and sometimes he put extra information in. He would say a little about a lot to reduce the seriousness or he would say a lot about a little to increase its importance.

Often what appears to be lying is someone's attempt to rectify a position which he sees as having been mismanaged by someone else. This is a sign of immaturity. The child sees an opportunity to behave dishonestly and hasn't understood a moral code.

Laurie's parents were horrified when they realised he had been stealing. He had been taking small amounts of money from lots of different places—his mum's bag, his sister's piggy bank and his father's trouser pocket. Laurie initially denied stealing and wailed that his parents didn't trust him. He said it was typical that he would be blamed and no-one ever thought it was anybody else's fault—only his.

His parents decided to double check and found proof that only Laurie could have taken money from a particular place in the house. When Laurie was confronted, he admitted to what he had done but said his parents still weren't being fair. He said he had no money, his parents had lots, he was part of their family and so he should have the same as them to spend on himself.

Laurie was too immature to see reality. He really believed that his parents' money should be for him. His parents' time, he felt, should be for him and his parents' possessions should be for him.

In order to work out a moral view many children will have experimented with what happens if:

- they eat the last piece of cake
- they take a packet of biscuits to their bedroom
- they specifically do something they have been told not to—run across a road, write on the wallpaper with invisible ink, cut their hair, experiment with their mother's makeup, play with someone else's toys or press the horn on the car

When children try something that they have been told not to do, you need to explain that there is a problem with what they have done. You need to explain you expect your child to be responsible so that you can trust that when she's left alone in the house, her brothers and sisters, the pets and even herself will all be safe when you return.

You can give her an example of something similar that happened to you when you were a child so she can see this as a learning process many people go through. If you can't think of one, look at the list above.

Teaching your child how to take responsibility for what she says can be as complicated as teaching her to take responsibility for what she does. Learning how to take your place in the world and cope with all the expectations and demands of a working, social and personal life is an ongoing activity. None of us knows how to cope or what to say in every situation, even when we are adult. Adults must expect to teach children how to cope with difficulties, rather than throw up their hands in horror when something the child does, shows there is something she needs to learn.

Some children will tell tall stories in order to communicate and feel part of an activity.

THE GIRL WHO TOLD A 'TALL' STORY

Karina was visiting her aunt over the weekend. Her aunt had to work on the Saturday morning. When she got back home she asked Karina what she had been doing. Karina was three and because she wanted to take part in a conversation with her aunt and she needed a familiar topic she said, 'I've been to play school.' Her aunt knew this wasn't true but continued with the conversation, asking next, 'What did you do?' Karina said that she had played with the plasticine. Karina's mum was also in the room so she asked Karina if she had had a night's sleep since play school. Karina thought and said, 'Yes, I have'.

Often what appear to be tall stories are really children's attempts to communicate and to cope with social demands beyond their maturity.

Learning how to take your place in the world and cope with all the expectations and demands of working life, social life and personal life is an ongoing activity.

Whingeing

DON'T PANIC

MAKING DECISIONS

HOW TO SUPPORT CHILDREN WHEN DECISIONS BACKFIRE

'I'm sick of my child not paying attention and being so frustrating.'

HAS YOUR CHILD EVER FRUSTRATED YOU BY:
- not being able to join in anything
- not being able to play on his own
- whingeing a lot
- always interrupting
- refusing everything that is offered

DON'T PANIC

You can find ways to help your child make the most of all opportunities, learn how to consider his behaviour and to change it so that he does not upset other people.

MAKING DECISIONS

Some children put themselves in a position from which they can't escape. They could be helped, but they feel they have too much invested in the way they behave to risk changing that behaviour. Gradually they forget that they had a choice and the awful behaviour becomes part of nearly everything they do.

THE GIRL WHOSE WORLD BECAME SMALLER AND SMALLER

Hannah's reputation at school and at home was that if she didn't want to do something, she would simply refuse to do it. She had a variety of strategies she used which she thought helped her avoid things, but actually they meant she kept missing out. Hannah's world became smaller and smaller. Everyone asked her before anything started whether she wanted to do it, and Hannah felt her reply had to be, 'No'. Hannah actually knew how to cope with some of the things that she felt uncertain about, but no-one ever helped her past her first step of saying 'No'. Hannah's parents were beside themselves because Hannah wouldn't go to other children's parties, speak to visitors or co-operate with anything the family was trying to do. Hannah wouldn't speak to her brother for days on end.

At school Hannah would bury her head in her arms every time there was new work to be done. She would never allow herself to think about what she could do, but would only allow herself to become panicked if the work was new. She was in danger of being ignored completely by the teacher because she rejected every effort the teacher made. The teacher, mindful of her responsibilities to all the other children, referred Hannah for special help.

How Hannah was helped

The special help that was offered was speech therapy. Everyone knew that Hannah could speak but the only available help that had anything to do with her refusal to speak was speech therapy. Hannah refused to speak at speech therapy and the problem did not go away.

She was then offered counselling and a series of activities were tried. The counsellor suggested reasons for Hannah's distress and Hannah agreed with quite a few of them. She said she had been bullied at school, she did find the work difficult and she had no friends. She said her mum and dad only liked her brother and he was given special things and her mum and dad were always having arguments.

Hannah's parents were made to feel that they had caused Hannah's problems and Hannah could believe that as well. The whole situation escalated. Hannah had to keep refusing to do anything. She had to keep thinking of things that frightened her. In the end Hannah had no relief from these negative reactions. She had completely lost her sense of herself as being someone who could do things and who could get pleasure out of them.

Counselling hadn't succeeded, so Hannah's parents decided that a change of school might work. They found a school which was interested in helping children who were stuck. This was an ordinary school where most of the children just had the normal range of childhood experiences—divorce, death of a family member, illness, unemployment and relocation.

Hannah continued to behave as if everything was frightening and difficult. She made people feel it would be cruel if anyone expected her to do anything she didn't want to. Hannah was never embarrassed by her behaviour.

Her teacher, however, noticed that occasionally Hannah's face would light up a little when certain activities were happening. They were always activities which another child had sparked off. One particular instance was when a child rushed out of the toilets to tell the teacher that there was a pencil in the toilet bowl. This caused great hilarity in the classroom and everyone thought of reasons for the pencil being in the bowl. As the teacher moved to sort out the problem, she noticed Hannah had a tiny smile. When she came back she wrote, up on the board, the reasons the children had come up with for the pencil being in the toilet. They wrote their own stories for just ten minutes. The children then read them out and Hannah's smile got bigger. The next day the children were still laughing about the toilet incident and thoroughly enjoyed listening to the teacher telling them a story about a goldfish being flushed down the toilet. The teacher asked all the children to put their heads down on the table while she told the story. She didn't draw attention to Hannah but because everyone was now doing what Hannah did, Hannah was part of the group completely. When the story finished the children began their day's school work. Some were doing maths, some reading and some finishing off their project. For the first time since Hannah had come to that school, she went and got her own work and sat down to do it.

For the first time since Hannah had come to that school she got a sticker for good work.

For the first time since Hannah had been going to school she had something to say about her day when she got home.

There were still times when Hannah would try out her old behaviour, but she enjoyed being part of the group most of the time and gradually all the old behaviour disappeared.

What Hannah's parents did

Hannah's parents stopped asking Hannah whether she wanted to do things and began to plan things that Hannah would have to do. Instead of saying, 'Do you want to go to Nana's?' they said, 'We are all going to Nana's; what are you going to take?' If Hannah answered, 'Nothing,' that didn't affect whether they went on the outing or not.

Hannah's parents had always assumed that they should give Hannah a choice whenever a decision had to be made. They had given her choices that were too difficult for a small child to make.

She had become overwhelmed by the difficulty and had shut herself off. When she was given choices which only meant her selecting an option within a menu of options she could handle that, and gradually could extend her possibilities. For example instead of being asked, 'What do you want to drink?' she was asked, 'Would you like a drink of orange or milk or water?'

Even adults find it impossible to answer some questions. If you are visiting a friend and you are asked what you would like for lunch you have no idea what they have in their cupboard or what they have to spare. As an adult you will probably ask, 'What is there?' or 'What have you got?' or you might say, 'Just a sandwich,' knowing that most people could manage that.

As adults we need to remember children haven't had enough experiences to know which answer to give in every situation. We need to help them.

Give them practice at making decisions within a framework.

Don't ask yes/no questions such as, 'Do you want to help me with the washing up?' If there really isn't a choice don't ask the question in that manner. Instead say, 'Do you want to wash the dishes while I dry them or shall I wash and you dry them?'

As adults we need to remember children haven't had enough experiences to know what to do in every situation. You need to help them by supporting them when a decision backfires.

HOW TO SUPPORT CHILDREN WHEN DECISIONS BACKFIRE

Helen was eight and playing in the garden with some friends. She picked up a rake and was pretending she was Boadicea. In her enthusiasm, she clipped one of her friends on the shoulder. The child started to cry. Helen panicked and climbed a tree. The other children went to get Helen's mother and she sorted out the problem and looked after the injured child. She went to the bottom of the tree and told Helen the child was all right and when Helen came down she would speak with her. Her tone of voice was calm, supportive without minimising the seriousness of the accident.

Helen chose to stay in the tree all afternoon. When she eventually came down her mum discussed with her how to avoid having an accident like that again. After this, Helen never climbed a tree when she had done something silly. There was no pay off for Helen up in the tree. The other children in the garden had continued to play. Helen was able to look on, but it was her choice not to take part. This may have been a choice she had regretted or it may have been a way of dealing with her embarrassment, but her mother's action meant she wouldn't get trapped into making that sort of choice again.

Christopher saved for a long time to buy a sweatshirt. When it was washed the colours ran. His dad explained to him how to check for colour fastness next time and also told him that sometimes things you buy aren't as good as you had hoped they would be.

Tracy's friend let her down. Her sister explained to her that all through her life she would be meeting people who may turn into long-term friends or the friendship might only last for a short while.

Mark was excited to be doing history at school until he started the course. The course turned out to be something he was not happy doing. His mum explained to him his options. He could:

- find out the procedure for changing the course. It may well be possible to change but you will have to do some finding out first
- look at the benefits of finishing the course, rather than abandoning it
- try to find ways of making the course more manageable

Talk to your children about decisions you have made that have been successful and others that have backfired.

It is important that children know that life is a continuous process of decision making. It would be impossible to make every choice with total vision. We all know the expression, 'With the benefit of hindsight.'

JOHN COULD BE SO EXASPERATING

John was impossible to live with. John had worked out that he would never have to do anything he didn't want to if he whinged, or if he went limp and did everything as sloppily as he could. However if he was interested then he would be on the ball.

At school John was always quick to notice an advantage he thought had been given to someone else like a chance to play or a new book. He never seemed to notice why an advantage had been given, like finishing work early or completing the last book.

At home John could turn a pleasant situation into a situation that was so fraught everyone just wanted it to end.

His parents, his teachers and his friends' parents tried everything they could to help him stop whingeing but nothing worked. Whenever John took part in an activity he did not want to do, he would do it sloppily. It was as if he lost control over his limbs and could not sit up. He seemed to have no energy for the task he was doing. He would write badly, slouch and yawn. Nothing anyone said could jolt him out of this state. Everyone knew there was another John because when he talked about football, which he was interested in, he was alert, entertaining and knowledgeable. At school John seemed prepared to talk, but not to write.

How John learned to stop whingeing

John was invited to his cousin's birthday party. As usual John flopped and whinged, moaned and slouched. When the children were eating John complained it wasn't fair because he did not have as many chips as everyone else. He flopped across the table knocking over people's drinks.

When the children were playing Pass the Parcel, John whined when he had to pass the parcel on. At the end of the party John stayed on with his parents for a barbecue. During the barbecue, his uncle suggested they watch the video of the party. Everyone was excited—looking out for themselves and commenting as the video was played. John started laughing like everyone else, but gradually became quieter and quieter. He suddenly realised what people meant when they complained about him. There on the screen, was someone John did not like. His parents noticed he had gone quiet.

That night when John had gone to bed they talked about whether seeing himself on a video might help John change his behaviour. Maybe he had realised what people meant when they complained about him. Certainly, the next morning John seemed to be more aware of the sound of his voice and did not whinge as much.

John continued to improve. It seemed he had worked out for himself how to stop whingeing. He became more co-operative and his parents found it possible to talk to him about why it was important he didn't slop about.

Sometimes it is possible for children to see themselves as others do and to use all the help you have given them to sort out the problem.

Life is a continuous process of decision making. Talk to your children about decisions you have made that have been successful and others that have backfired.

Being cruel

DON'T PANIC

HOW TO THINK ABOUT BEHAVIOUR AND NOT JUST
WORRY ABOUT IT

HOW TO PROTECT OTHERS

'I'm sick of my child not paying attention, and hurting me.'

HAS YOUR CHILD EVER HURT YOU BY:
- saying horrible things?
- doing horrible things?

Don't panic

Remember, children love their parents and want to be loved by them. If they are doing something cruel, it will be because there is something they don't understand. Your child will not be properly aware of the effect her behaviour is having. She is learning and will need to try things out. Your first priority must be to protect anyone or anything who is vulnerable. Your child needs you to give her careful explanations of other things she could have said and other things she could have done and things she should never do. Then she will have the chance to make up for the upset she has caused. She will also have the chance of learning how to behave in an acceptable way—now and in the future.

THE GIRL WHO THOUGHT IT WAS ALL RIGHT TO HURT ANIMALS AND CHILDREN

Margaret hurt her dog when she beat it on the head with a stick. The family were horrified. When she threw the tadpoles around the classroom at school, adults and children were appalled. Whenever Margaret went missing, which she often did, people were terrified that she would be damaging or destroying something else. In the playground Margaret picked on smaller children. Margaret's behaviour was making her more and more isolated. No one wanted her near them—not the teachers nor the children. Everyone felt powerless to help. No-one knew what to do.

Margaret had been seen by psychologists but they could shed no light on her difficulties. They did arrange for her to go to a special school where she would be in a smaller class and have closer supervision. There was no advice about what could be done at home. Margaret didn't settle at the new school. Her teachers told Margaret's mother that Margaret didn't have the sort of learning difficulty that they were used to dealing with—she just had a behaviour problem.

Margaret's mum was desperate. She had three other children and they were fine but Margaret was a complete mystery to her. She was frightened of her and for her.

What Margaret's mother did

One evening, Margaret's mum was listening to the radio when she heard a story about a young boy who sounded so similar to Margaret it was uncanny. This boy had no friends and said he was going to do terrible things to people like cutting out his sister's eyeballs and putting them in the dustbin. His parents had bought him white mice so he would have something to care about and he did seem very attached to them. His mother was devastated when she found him one day feeding them to the cat.

The experts on the program said that he had 'Asperger's Syndrome' but didn't give any advice.

> Asperger's Syndrome is seen as a less severe form of autism where the sufferer tries to make social contact but hasn't the skills to engage in a relationship at any level. The person with Asperger's Syndrome is considered to have no understanding of how social situations work and so his behaviour may be impulsive, uncaring or rude.

As Margaret's mum listened she became angry when she realised that the little boy's problems had been ignored by the experts once they had labelled them. Just like her, the boy's mother was offered no help and no hope.

What she felt should have happened was every time the mother described a problem there should have been at least one practical suggestion in reply. Gardening programs often have a panel of people who all answer the same question in different ways depending on their experience and knowledge. The questioner can then think about the advice given, and apply whatever seems appropriate to their particular situation. That same format would be helpful whenever a program devoted to behaviour problems was broadcast. People who ask questions about a problem, want suggestions on what they can do to reduce the problem or overcome it. They don't want the problem named and then ignored. That simply leaves them feeling desperate and hopeless. They need to feel empowered to use what they already know and what they have now been told so they can make progress.

Margaret's mother wrote a letter to the program makers expressing her anger. She explained what it felt like to have a child whom no-one could cope with and how programs like theirs should try to give parents of children with behaviour problems a sense of direction and hope.

When Margaret's mother came to see us we gave her the following guidelines for thinking about children who are cruel. The most important thing is that parents realise they can think about the behaviour and not just worry about it. To think clearly you need to observe closely.

HOW TO THINK ABOUT BEHAVIOUR AND NOT JUST WORRY ABOUT IT

When parents are worried about the behaviour of their children they need to know:

Is the behaviour normal?

Most parents only know a few children, so their knowledge of what is normal and what isn't, is based on extremely limited experience. Sometimes the behaviour which is labelled as abnormal, is actually occurring to some extent or other in a large number of children in the group.

What else should you look for?

Often when there is a problem it is only the poor behaviour of the child that is noticed. Make a list of things she can do that don't embarrass or alarm you. For example:

CAN SHE:
1. Take part in conversations nicely?   Not always, but sometimes.
2. Join in a game fairly?   Not always, but sometimes.

3. Buy something in a shop successfully?   Not always, but sometimes.

4. Help clear the table quickly?   Not always, but sometimes.

5. Look after the pets carefully?   Not always, but sometimes.

6. Play with smaller children responsibly?   Not always, but sometimes.

7. Play with older children appropriately?   Not always, but sometimes.

These are just a few areas to look at. It is important to appreciate that everyone can do some things well some of the time. If we only notice the things which have not been done well we may be misled into believing a child is a hopeless case, rather than an individual who is learning different things at different times just like everyone else. This doesn't mean that unacceptable behaviour can be left. It does mean that your child has shown she is capable of learning. So therefore is capable of being taught what she now needs to know.

HOW TO PROTECT OTHERS
Children who are cruel to vulnerable creatures need help so that they can learn to be kind. They should always be accompanied when they are in a position where they might be cruel because the first consideration is always to protect those that are vulnerable. Secondly it is important to take every opportunity to teach children how to care sensibly and appropriately. To help your child learn, take her to places where animals, are looked after so she can see how people care for animals and that the care of animals is so important it is somebody's job (farms, zoos, pet corners and pet shops).

If your child is cruel to smaller children, take her to a park and watch how older people look after younger ones. Talk to her about things you see and discuss how your child could behave if she was looking after or playing with a younger child.

Make sure your child realises which things are appropriate for her to do with a small child and which things are dangerous. For example, if you have a six year old who is learning to play with smaller children, explain that playing a catching or kicking game with a ball is safe and fun. However, taking a smaller child down to look at the ducks in an unprotected pond is dangerous. It is useful to point out to your child some of her own games that have age limits on them so she can see that being aware of safety is someone's responsibility.

Many children will do cruel things until they learn that an animal or a vulnerable child needs their care. Curiosity has to be tempered with caution and responsibility.

If a child has reached an age where this caution and responsibility should have been understood and it hasn't been, then there is something the child hasn't picked up just from being alive. The child will have to be taught it. For many children the understanding that vulnerable creatures need their care has been taught at just the time they were ready to understand it. This means that gentleness can appear to be natural—the child was born gentle rather than taught how to behave towards vulnerable creatures. 'Nature red in tooth and claw' is a difficult concept. Children who are being taught to care need to understand a cat pouncing on a mouse and playing with it before killing and eating it can be horrifying but natural. A bully bullying her victim is unacceptable. The bully is a human and she should be thinking about the consequences of her behaviour.

Human beings have ways of being together which mean everyone is safe. The child just has to learn these ways.

You can teach your child how to think about her actions.

When Margaret's mother tried these things she found that they worked. She was able to talk to Margaret and Margaret was fascinated by the discussion.

It is important to take every opportunity to teach children how to care sensibly and appropriately.

Bullying

DON'T PANIC

WHAT TO DO IF YOU HAVE A CHILD WHO NEEDS TO
LEARN HOW TO LEARN

WHAT TO DO IF YOU HAVE A CHILD WHO NEEDS TO
LEARN APPLICATION

'I'm sick of my child not paying attention and making me feel a complete idiot.'

HAS YOUR CHILD EVER MADE YOU FEEL A COMPLETE IDIOT BY:

- arguing and refusing to do what you've asked him?
- always blaming you for something he's done?
- always looking for an excuse so he doesn't have to take responsibility?
- bullying you or anyone else if he doesn't get his own way?
- speaking to you so rudely that your natural reaction is to say no, even if what he was wanting was reasonable?

When people have been bullied they feel diminished, dominated and desperate. Bullying includes physical abuse, verbal attacks, social rejection, gossip and anything else that makes someone feel intimidated.

In our experience, the easiest bullying to overcome is the physical. It is obvious when it has been done and it doesn't take long to explain to the child other ways of dealing with frustration. It is harder to deal with bullying when it is done by a child who threatens to put himself or someone else in danger when he doesn't get his own way or is not centre stage. Sometimes parents feel if they tackle this form of bullying they may stamp out their child's individuality. In fact, when they unpick behaviour that makes other people feel uncomfortable, they reveal the true personality of their child. They are relieved and so is their child.

DON'T PANIC

You can teach your child how to speak so that he can get what he wants without making everyone else feel worthless.

You can teach your child that anyone can say no, including you. People might say yes if they feel they are being treated with respect.

You can teach your child that he doesn't have to be angry about mistakes. Mistakes do happen.

You can show him how mistakes can be sorted out quickly if there is co-operation not confrontation.

You can teach your children they are not in competition with others. They are really just learning something. Sometimes they will learn faster than other people, sometimes they will be in the middle and sometimes they will be the slowest. The important thing is they are improving their skills and learning all the time.

You can teach your child not to feel oppressed by life. He will be doing well if he has done something better or faster or more easily than he has done it before.

THE BOY WHO FRIGHTENED HIS PARENTS

Whenever Mark was asked to do something he didn't want to do he would lose his temper. It didn't matter how reasonable the request was he would fly off the handle. The whole family felt as if they were walking on cracked eggs. Mark would frighten his parents by talking about drugs or alcohol. He always implied that he was able to get hold of both of them. He was constantly threatening his parents by insinuating that if he didn't get what he wanted he would go off the rails. His parents were alarmed because Mark was starting secondary school in a few months and they didn't want him to go in with a bad reputation. They kept giving in. They knew they shouldn't but every time they tried to stand up to him he made life a misery.

Mark had been born while his mother was still a student and he had been looked after by several baby minders. His mother wondered whether all his problems stemmed from this time.

His dad thought the problems started when Mark began school at five. Two weeks after starting school his sister was born and his mum hadn't worked for three years.

His gran thought that Mark was missing his grandad who had died in a car accident two years earlier. Mark had been good friends with his grandad. They had done a lot together.

For some time everyone had thought that Mark would just grow out of his frightening behaviour but it was now obvious that wasn't going to happen.

Whatever the reason for the problem it had to be sorted out and quickly.

One night after a particularly bad screaming fit Mark burst into tears. Everyone was so worn out by the tension of his tantrum that when he cried he was sent to bed. His parents sat down exhausted trying to decide what to do next.

His dad decided the first thing he had to do was tell Mark that his behaviour was making everyone miserable. When he went into Mark's bedroom to talk to him Mark was lying on his bed staring at the ceiling. As his dad caught sight of his expression he suddenly remembered something. When he was Mark's age and he was due to move up to Secondary School he was terrified. He decided to ask Mark how he felt about the change of schools. At first Mark just grunted and refused to answer but his dad persisted and gently asked him different questions.

Gradually Mark went from grunting to muttering and his dad went from feeling totally fed up with him to being curious to see if he could get Mark to talk. He realised that if he could get the questions right he would be able to help Mark. He became interested in the questions he was asking Mark as his own memories of being Mark's age flooded back. He asked lots of questions, some of which Mark muttered replies to and some which made Mark turn his head to the wall. It became obvious that Mark was worried about moving up to Secondary School.

His dad asked what he thought was a fairly simple question about what Mark was looking forward to doing in the lunchtime. Suddenly Mark fired back a very angry reply. Mark's dad felt huge disappointment. He wondered whether to leave Mark alone or keep going. He decided to keep going and continued to ask questions about lunchtime. What had Mark heard happened, at the school, in the lunch break?

Who had told him what lunchtimes would be like?

Mark said his friend, Danny, had a brother at the school and he had told him all about how terrible the lunchtimes were. He had told him how new children would be picked on and made to fight with older children. Mark's father asked Mark whether Danny was frightened about lunchtimes. Mark said Danny wasn't because his brother had said he might let him play with his gang.

Mark's dad smiled with relief. He recognised what Mark was going through and knew he would be able to help him.

Mark was tired and his dad suggested he go to sleep. His dad went back to talk to Mark's mum. He explained that Mark's bad tempers were because he was really frightened about what he was going to do at his new school at lunchtimes and Mark felt he wasn't going to be able to cope.

They discussed what they should do next. Should they buy him a present or take him out for a treat to help him forget his worries? Mark's mum said although she felt that would be a nice idea to give him a treat it was more important that Mark knew they were always there to help sort out his problems.

When Mark got up they sat and talked with him about what he felt he had learned by talking with his dad. At first Mark sounded as if he didn't understand what the question meant but gradually he began to see he had learned a lot.

What Mark had learned
- If he buried a problem he got into trouble for all sorts of other things.
- His mum and dad did care about him and were interested in helping him try to sort out his problems.
- Just because somebody told you something was going to be hard it didn't have to be frightening. It could be interesting working out how to do it.

What Mark's parents learned
- Mark had been desperately frightened.
- Next time Mark behaved dreadfully they would try to find a cause in his everyday life instead of thinking his behaviour was because of his early life and there was nothing they could do about it.

Although all Mark's dreadful behaviour may not have been only due to him worrying about changing school, any time he was under pressure he was likely to take his frustrations out on everyone else.

Mark could be taught how to find ways of coping with stress.

THE BOYS WHO BLAMED THEIR PARENTS BECAUSE THEY THOUGHT LIFE SHOULD BE EASY

Sandy and Luke were similar. They were never satisfied. They would get into muddles about where they wanted to be and what they wanted to do. They always felt that they weren't as good as everyone

else. Anything they were good at they discounted. They would say—
'Everybody can do that', or shrug if someone praised them. If their
parents told them how much they loved them, that was ignored. If
they were feeling unhappy they would blame their parents for not
loving them enough.

They were always saying they weren't doing as well as everyone
else at school but when their parents and teachers decided on a
program which would help overcome the problem, Luke and Sandy
just wanted a miracle cure.

Sandy complained that his artwork was dreadful. Everyone else
could draw. He was the only one in the class who couldn't. He was
allowed extra time at lunchtime to practise his drawing with help from
the teacher. His drawing improved. Sandy was pleased at first but two
weeks later he was telling his parents again that he couldn't draw.

Luke had to write a book review. His mum helped him and Luke
seemed happy that he knew what to do and went off to do it.

Luke's mother got a 'phone call from his teacher saying that
Luke had been in tears at school because he couldn't do his book
review. Luke's mother was flabbergasted, confused and hurt. She
felt as if the teacher thought it was her fault.

Luke and Sandy both seemed to carry a picture in their head of
themselves being able to do everything and know everything. They did
not seem to have a picture of themselves learning how to do things.

What to do if you have a child like Sandy or Luke

Every time they achieve something you write it down or get them
to write it down.

The achievements can be quite commonplace—answering the
'phone nicely, riding up a hill without getting off, learning the
eight times table.

Every time your child is despondent about his abilities, list what
it is that he is upset about and then break the activity down into
small parts so he can tick them off as he learns to do each one.

For example, I want to be able to do nice handwriting might be
broken down into:

- do 'f's
- join up a and s
- leave the same size gap between words

- have all the letters slanting the same way
- join r up to other letters

Then ask him to select the one he is going to start with. It is the inability to be selective which causes some children so much distress. They think they should be able to 'eat the elephant in one bite' rather than being able to nibble away at it until eventually it has all gone.

THE CHILD THAT BROUGHT THE WORST OUT IN EVERYONE

Tom, when he was in primary school, had always got good marks. Success had come to him easily so he had never learned how to apply himself to any task. If it didn't come easily, it didn't come at all.

He had aptitude but no application. Aptitude is the ability to grasp an idea very quickly. Application is the ability to work at something which you haven't been able to grasp quickly. Then you learn to use that idea on its own or to put it together with other ideas to develop understanding and skills.

When Tom got to secondary school, his lack of application meant that he had to find ways of disguising his poor performance when the work became difficult. He became laid back, cynical and dismissive of any requests for greater effort. His classmates knew he was cleverer than they were because he would always know answers to any questions that were based on the lesson they had just been doing. His marks were not as high as many people in his class but he was so arrogant that he traded on his ability to give a clever answer out loud and never bothered about the skills he needed to have in order to get higher marks.

Tom was quick to distract the class by making sly comments and rude remarks. Teachers dreaded talking about some topics or having to use some words when Tom was in the room. Other children were frightened of him because he used his verbal ability to belittle teachers, pupils, his friends, his family—in fact anyone.

A child like Tom always keeps himself on safe ground. Since he never risks anything he reduces the chance that he will make a mistake. He would rather do nothing new than, in his mind, be caught out getting something wrong. He doesn't recognise risks other people take. Because he only does one thing at a time he is oblivious to the real situation that you have to:

- organise yourself
- set your own priorities
- make mistakes
- forgive yourself
- move on

What to do if you have a child like Tom

You need to set up situations where he can't tell at the beginning what he will be expected to do at the end. His arrogant behaviour won't work if he can't be sure what he has to produce at the end.

It may take several attempts before he switches from his old strategies, which will fail, to learning the new strategies which will give him success.

Start with a subject he is interested in and thinks he knows a lot about and give him an article to read on that subject. Now get him to write something about what he has read. Check what he has written against the article and jot down points he has not covered.

Write a keyword, from the article, for each point and ask him to see if he can improve what he has already written by covering the extra points.

While he is getting on, you should be doing the same thing so that you explore together. He will see you having to think hard about possibilities which he won't have a ready answer for either.

You might have something else you can do like tidying up a garage—each of you writes a plan and then compares notes. Has he considered something you have missed? Has he left something out which would need to be done?

BY WORKING WITH HIM YOU:

- stop him bamboozling you with glib answers
- slow the pace down to a point where discussion can take place
- help him realise that 'cover all' responses rarely pick up the detail needed to achieve progress. That attitude means you can be stuck at the same level for ever

10 POINTS TO REMEMBER

1. Talk to other people who have difficult children—then you will realise it's not only you.
2. Remind yourself of all the things you are good at—make a list.
3. Every day is a new learning experience for every parent.
4. You can be a brilliant parent of a child when he is one age and flounder completely with the same child at a different age.
5. Remind yourself of what you were like when you were the same age but don't think the present situation is necessarily the same as the one you were in.
6. Listening to what others think of your child as an individual is very important.
7. Whenever there is a problem there will be as many solutions suggested as there are people suggesting them.
8. For best results see each day as a new starting point and each situation afresh.
9. Look at the list of things you are good at.
10. Use the relaxations.

Worrying behaviour

DON'T PANIC

WHAT TO DO ABOUT CONSTANT COMPLAINING

'WHAT HAPPENED IN SCHOOL TODAY?' 'NOTHING.'

5 TIPS FOR TEACHING SOMEONE HOW TO LEARN

'I'm sick of my child not paying attention and making me feel so hopeless.'

HAS YOUR CHILD EVER MADE YOU FEEL THAT YOU ARE A HOPELESS PARENT BY:

- refusing to eat
- looking neglected
- having everyone feeling sorry for her
- being lovely for someone else and dreadful for you

DON'T PANIC

Your child may just need guidance to change from a child who looks as though her parents can't cope with her, to a child who looks as though she is cherished. However, some children are more difficult to change—they can be manipulative. To help any child to change you first need to find out how she is thinking. By observing your child and finding out what she is thinking, you will be able to tell whether she needs long-term help, or just a few suggestions.

WHAT TO DO ABOUT CONSTANT COMPLAINING

THE GIRL WHO WAS DREADFUL TO HER MUM

Helen's mum felt completely exhausted within seconds of picking Helen up from school. No matter how determined she was to be bright and cheerful when she met her daughter, the sight of Helen dragging her feet across the playground and looking fed up drained every last bit of energy from her. What was so upsetting was that the only time Helen looked as dreadful as this was when she was with her mum. With everyone else she was cheerful, charming and chatty.

Helen's mum had tried bringing treats with her when she met Helen to make her happy but it hadn't worked. Helen began to demand more and more. She never said thank you and would often be so careless with a toy or book she had been given that it broke and if the treat was food she would just take a couple of bites and throw the rest away.

Helen's parents had split up a year ago and her dad had gone to live with another woman and her daughter who was Helen's age. Helen visited her dad in his new house and was never difficult on these visits but was back to her old behaviour with her mum the minute she got home.

How Helen's mum tried to find some answers

When Helen's mum talked to her friends, she found that some of them were having similar problems with their children, too. Although she had been worried that Helen's behaviour was caused by the family breaking up, not all the children who were being difficult had suffered major problems like this.

Occasionally Helen and her mum would have a lovely time together, but Helen all too quickly would change, and usually her mum couldn't work out why.

To add to her confusion, Helen's mum couldn't remember ever having spoken rudely to her own mother. Her own father had died when she was a child and she and her sisters had always respected their mum and knew that they had to pull their weight. She couldn't understand why Helen seemed to hate her and constantly complained. Helen never showed any appreciation for anything her mother did.

One day when Helen's mum had made her daughter's favourite meal Helen pulled a face and said she wasn't going to eat any because she hated it. Helen's mum was so exhausted she began to cry She left the room and lay on her bed sobbing. Gradually the feelings of despair changed to determination to sort the problem out. Helen had gone too far. She was now complaining even when it was obvious she had no need to. Helen's mum realised she was being used as a doormat and that she would have to tackle the problem for her own sake as well as Helen's.

She calmly returned to the table where Helen was just finishing her meal.

Let's try and find some possibilities

Helen's mum said she was glad that Helen had been able to finish her meal because she was sure she must have been hungry. She added that she had made that meal because she knew it was Helen's favourite and the best thing now would be for them to sit down and work out a list of things Helen was happy to eat. Then she would write down the things she liked and together they could draw up a menu of meals for the whole week.

Helen agreed and they had a reasonable time making the list. At the end of the discussion Helen seemed quite taken with the idea of writing down possibilities. Her mum said they could try it again sometime.

From now on, any time Helen was rude, her mum would think of a way of getting them both out of the hole by saying, 'Tell you what Helen, let's try and find some possibilities.'

This approach seemed to work. Helen had a chance of letting her mum know what her new preferences were. She became more communicative and the number of times she was sullen became fewer. Helen was lucky. Her mum was able to make sure Helen was never stuck with her immature response to frustration. Helen was learning communication skills which would help her through the rest of her life.

Helen's mum also realised that she had to put limits on the way Helen treated her. She had thought a good mother should be able to keep her child happy. Now she realised a good parent could use any difficulty at home to teach their children how to handle frustration or their responsibilities in the outside world.

'WHAT HAPPENED AT SCHOOL TODAY?' 'NOTHING.'

Matthew was one of those children who made his dad feel as if he needed to be a member of the secret service in order to find out what Matthew had done at school or wherever he had been.

You can often have the feeling as a parent when children tell you they've done 'nothing' that never has so much time been allowed for so many to do so little! Of course they haven't done 'nothing', but just how do you find out what they have done?

These questions worked for Matthew's dad

1. Did your teacher shout today? Or, who did the teacher shout at today?
2. Did anything funny happen today?
3. Did you see any blood at school today?

4. Did your teacher say anything about his pets today?
5. Did anyone break a school rule today?
6. What was the best bit about today?
7. Was there a worst bit about school today?

ANOTHER TACK TO TAKE IS:
What was the loudest, quietest, funniest, strangest, noisiest, messiest, tastiest or smelliest thing that happened today?

OR YOU COULD TRY:
When did you feel—happy, proud, clever, silly, sensible, shy or confident today?

Some children find it very difficult to know how to behave when they are picked up by a parent after they have been involved in another activity like—school, playing with friends, a party, sports club, guides, cubs or scouts etc.

When you pick up your child and she is being silly—giggling or fooling around; withdrawn or surly or seems extremely uncommunicative you need to find out what she has been doing. Then you will know whether she just can't cope with changing from one activity to another, or whether she is really distressed.

PEOPLE WILL THINK THAT I JUST DON'T CARE

Susan often looked like she hadn't washed for a week and she'd been to bed in her clothes. Even at thirteen she didn't seem to be taking any more interest in her appearance. She would drag her feet as she walked, scuffing her shoes along the ground. She would mumble if she was spoken to. Her clothes were always half hanging off. When she sat down she sprawled and let her hair fall over her eyes.

Her mum bought her clothes and always carefully washed and ironed her school uniform. But Susan still managed to look like a ragamuffin by the time she had got out of the car to go into school.

At first her mum nagged her to brush her hair, wash her face, brush her teeth but then she decided that by thirteen Susan should be taking more responsibility for this herself. An ideal opportunity presented itself.

How Susan's mum helped Susan look after herself

Susan's form was going away on a school camp. She was given a list of things to take and her mum told her that she would have to be responsible for packing her own bag. She knew it was important that Susan take responsibility for her own belongings and for making sure that everything she needed was packed.

Susan's mother was determined that Susan would be able to look after herself, take pride in her appearance and have the skills for making sure she presented herself well. She knew that people who hadn't been taught how to present themselves well, rarely worked it out on their own.

The first problem Susan had was finding clothes in the muddle that was her bedroom! Her mum resisted the temptation to moan about the state of the room and instead asked Susan what plans she had made for taking care of her belongings when she was away.

When Susan looked surprised she explained that if all the children have their clothes lying about on the floor, it would be easy for things to get muddled up. Susan hadn't thought about it and her mum suggested she pack a plastic bag for her dirty washing. She also drew Susan's attention to the problem of looking after valuables. They decided on things Susan would take and things she could leave behind because she would be too upset if they were lost. They thought about clothes for different weather conditions and discussed what was sensible to take.

Although when Susan came home from the school camp she still looked like a ragamuffin, she did seem to have a much greater understanding about looking after herself and her possessions.

THE BOY WHO STOPPED EATING

Grant looked ill. When it came to mealtimes he couldn't be persuaded to eat. His concentration was poor. It had never been particularly good but now he wasn't eating it was terrible. His parents felt sure that if he would eat sensibly he would be able to concentrate. They took him to the doctor and he said Grant shouldn't be forced to eat and he should be allowed to choose:

- *when to eat*
- *what to eat*
- *how much to eat*

For the next week every mealtime became a drama.
- *Would Grant choose anything to eat?*
- *If he chose it would he eat it?*
- *If he ate it would he eat enough?*

How Grant's family solved the problem

At first his parents were happy to try what the doctor had suggested, but after a while they found it tiresome. They were sick of having meal times, when they felt they should have been able to relax and unwind, turned into fraught events. To break the tension, they arranged to visit a friend's home for a meal without Grant and told him that his uncle was coming to look after him. His uncle would bring his own meal and Grant could help himself to the food in the cupboard or in the refrigerator. They made no fuss about any particular food for Grant, although there was plenty there. The first time they went out Grant ate nothing—he just looked mournful. His uncle refused to feel sorry for him and so did his parents.

Grant's parents planned another meal out, and made the same arrangements. However, this time Grant did eat—not very much, but at least he chose something and ate it. Grant's uncle stayed the night and in the morning the two of them had breakfast together. Grant seemed relaxed and ate well.

The third time Grant's parents went out and his uncle came was different. This time Grant told his uncle that he had stopped eating because he had heard people say if you couldn't concentrate it might be because you didn't eat enough. He knew he didn't concentrate and thought that if he stopped eating that would explain it and everyone would stop worrying.

Grant was not suffering from anorexia. He had just put himself into a ridiculous position. His refusal to eat was, he thought, a way of explaining his inability to concentrate. If he was hungry he stopped concentrating altogether. Once he started eating properly again, he found he was able to concentrate in school better than he ever had before.

At first Grant had to use a lot of self control to make himself eat. He began to notice sometimes, when he wasn't hungry, he found it hard to concentrate. Then he noticed that if the work was difficult he stopped concentrating because he was panicking.

He also noticed that other people found concentrating all the time difficult as well. He recognised that other people had different reasons for poor concentration. His academic work improved because he made sure he had enough to eat and asked for help when he found something difficult.

THE BOY WHO GOT STUCK

Chris, at thirteen, couldn't read very well. He was convinced he shouldn't be expected to read and he wouldn't practise reading. He was sure that all the difficulties he had in moving house, moving school, changing dads meant that no-one should expect him to read. At school he made friends with Steven who had spent a lot of time in hospital because of his asthma. Both boys received special help from the school.

How Chris learned how to learn

When Steven began to make progress, Chris started to panic. Steven was his friend and he didn't want him to improve because then he might leave the special help group and leave Chris as well. Chris' mum explained that the solution was for Chris to start to improve too. She said that Steven had also missed a lot of school and had to cope with many changes, but he had managed to start to learn. Chris didn't have to think that just because he'd had lots of problems he would never be able to learn. Chris began to cry and sobbed that he couldn't learn—that he did try but he just couldn't do it. His step-dad asked if Chris wanted his help. Chris said he did.

WHEN THEY BEGAN TO WORK CHRIS COULDN'T:
- look at the book
- listen to what was being asked
- believe he could do anything

This sort of behaviour had always put people off helping him. They found they couldn't keep paying attention when Chris wouldn't pay attention.

His step-dad asked Chris to count the number of letters in each word on one page of his reading book. It was a book with about 150 words on each page. Chris believed he couldn't read this book but there was no way he could pretend he couldn't count the number of letters in a word. By giving Chris an activity he could do his step-dad was able to check on how he approached his work.

Every time Chris looked up, dropped his pencil, found an excuse for getting out of his seat, started a conversation, began to tap or hum or doodled on his page his step-dad told him what he was doing. His step-dad realised that as well as teaching Chris how to read properly he was teaching him how to learn.

5 TIPS FOR TEACHING SOMEONE HOW TO LEARN

1. Give a task that you know the child can do.
2. Sit where you can see the child doing it.
3. Each time the child stops, notice why.
4. If the interruption is because the child genuinely needs help—give help.
5. If the interruption is a distraction from the task, point out to the child that's what she's doing.

THE GIRL WHO ALWAYS GOT OUT OF HER WORK

Caroline was a past master at finding some reason for not getting on with what she was supposed to do. Every sound would catch her attention and she would use each sound as an excuse for stopping work.

Caroline had developed the art of finding things to do which appeared reasonable and which meant she didn't have to do what she'd been asked to do. She would go and get a rubber, put her used paper in the bin, tell someone something very important and put her pencil case in a safe place.

Improving Caroline's work

Caroline improved when over a five-minute period her older sister listed every reason Caroline gave for moving. Caroline's task after this was to try and reduce the list and increase the work.

This method is very successful at improving a child's attention span and should be continued until the child builds up a habit of getting on with her work rather than getting out of her work.

How to Cast the Magic Spell

1. Ask your child to find a word to try out. It can be any word. Your child doesn't have to be able to read it, just point to it.
2. Then your child can read out the letters to you.
3. Write the word out so that your child can see it.
4. Now ask what your child can see when looking at the word, and say what you can see.
5. Write down what you've both said you can see.
6. Now, if you haven't already noticed, look to see whether there are any double letters or letters repeated.
7. Now see if your child can spell the word out loud.
8. If so, see if he or she can spell it backwards.
9. If not, see where the mistake is being made and offer suggestions for how to memorise the word.
10. Now, try Step 7 again.

The Magic Spell works because children realise they can memorise words which they thought were too hard. When they thought they were stupid or couldn't spell, their energy was used up worrying, feeling frightened or helpless because they knew they wouldn't be able to hide the fact. After using the Magic Spell, their energy can be directed into learning spelling successfully. Instead of believing they can't, they now believe they can!

Anti-social behaviour

DON'T PANIC

TEACHING SHARING

STOPPING SQUABBLES

'I'm sick of my child not paying attention and making going out a nightmare.'

HAS YOUR CHILD EVER MADE GOING OUT A NIGHTMARE BY:

• sloppy eating
• having horrible manners
• fighting

DON'T PANIC

You can establish an atmosphere so that when you go out everyone will feel comfortable and relaxed. You just need to make sure you have taught your child what he needs to know.

Unless there is a physical difficulty, children are expected to eat appropriately for their age. If they can't, the natural reaction of everyone who comes in contact with them, when they are eating, will be astonishment, puzzlement and disgust. Peter's eating caused just such reactions.

PETER—THE CHILD NO-ONE WANTED AT THE TABLE

A doctor had explained to Peter's parents that problems at birth had left Peter with mild brain damage. Peter was the first child in his family, and his parents thought that anything he didn't learn to do naturally, he wouldn't be able to be taught because of the slight brain damage. They thought it would be unfair to put him under any pressure at all.

Peter didn't control his biting or chewing when he was eating. When his parents couldn't stand him sitting with them at the table and spitting the food out they put him into another room while they ate. They did take him to fast food restaurants because they felt he shouldn't be denied treats since his dreadful eating wasn't his fault.

Parents can find themselves in this position when an expert tells them their child has a problem. The expert doesn't give them any way to help overcome or modify the difficulties that can arise. The parents then assume that every single problem their child has, is as a result of the initial problem. In Peter's case the initial problem was mild brain damage. Other children may experience the same difficulty, but their parents will assume it is part of life. If you think something is part of life you will try to help your child learn how to do his best. If you think it is because of a problem you may excuse it rather than try to change it.

How Peter learned how to eat properly

When Peter started school his dreadful eating was seen as part of his condition. One day at lunchtime an assistant saw him eating and asked his teacher if she could try to help him improve.

First she watched what he did with the food. Because he didn't bite properly, he would push food into his mouth until his mouth was full. Then he would spit it out again. He would keep repeating this. The food quickly became a disgusting, soggy mush on his plate.

The assistant realised that Peter didn't know how to bite. She got some children to help her show him how biting happened. They each had a piece of bread and took it in turns to bite a bit off. Peter watched each child in turn. Then he had a go himself.

At first Peter couldn't manage biting at all, but gradually he learned how to do it. Soon he could bite and chew bread or a piece of apple. Within a week he could cope with eating most things.

TEACHING SHARING

THE BOY WHO HAD HORRIBLE MANNERS

Luke came from a home where his parents and his grandparents were very polite. When he went out, Luke was always grabbing toys from other children, snatching biscuits when they were offered and interrupting when other people were speaking.

It was obvious that Luke had seen people behave well. Whenever he was taken to one side to be told about his behaviour he would look contrite and be able to answer questions on what he should have done. These little 'talkings to' didn't change his behaviour at all. Whenever he returned to the game or the next time he was offered food it was just the same. It didn't seem to make any difference whether he knew anyone was watching him or not. Until he was pulled over and made to stop, he behaved as if he'd never been taught any manners at all.

Luke was quick to notice if other children were misbehaving. He would rush up to adults complaining that someone had done something wrong.

One day Luke was out with his family on a picnic. He was playing with some other children in the picnic area when suddenly, to the adults horror, Luke pushed a little girl roughly and she toppled to the ground. Luke's parents were aghast and so were the little girl's parents. Luke had pushed her over because she was about to pick up a ball and he thought she shouldn't. Luke's parents were very embarrassed and concerned. They apologised to the girl's parents and took Luke to one side. When they talked to him, although he looked very shamefaced, they knew that he wasn't really listening to them.

Teaching Luke to share

Shortly afterwards, the family were going out for the day in the car. Everyone had to help and take something to the car. Luke was asked to take the cool box. Luke jumped into the car and left the cool box by the front door. Luke's dad reminded him to get the cool box and told him to get out of the car and do it. Luke did get out of the car but explained the whole time that he needed to be in the car because he wanted a seat by the window. His dad told him again that he was to get the cool box, but Luke simply dived back into the car. This happened three times.

Luke's father was absolutely stunned by what was happening. It dawned on him Luke probably had no idea that he was being asked to do something. He certainly had no idea **why** he was being asked to do something. He didn't realise he was expected to help because he was part of the group. It was obvious that Luke had no idea that **what** his father was asking him to do was important. Luke's mind was full of what Luke wanted.

For the first time Luke's father realised why Luke played so roughly.

- If Luke was playing a game and wanted the ball, he had no idea that he had to take account of the fact that he was part of a group of people playing.
- If he wanted a biscuit off a plate, he had no idea as the biscuits would have to be shared, he should leave some.

• If he wanted to say something there was no point in anybody protesting that he was interrupting because Luke only saw what he wanted to say as what needed to be said.

Luke's dad had a flash of inspiration. He realised that Luke thought he was the only person who mattered. In Luke's opinion everybody else was simply there to service his needs. Up until that time, all the adults in Luke's life had thought that if they showed Luke how to behave well, took him aside when he behaved badly, and explained to him what he was doing wrong, he would learn how to behave properly. Luke had learned the words, but really had no idea what the words meant in terms of his behaviour. He needed to learn how to be part of a group.

4 things Luke needed to learn
• He was a person.
• He was a person amongst other people.
• People when they are in groups have to think differently than when they are on their own.
• When he was with other people he had to behave as if he was in a group.

Luke's father decided to help him by describing Luke's situation in terms of a picture. Every time Luke didn't understand what he needed to be doing, his dad would ask him who was in the picture. Gradually Luke realised that there was usually someone else in the picture and he had a different position in the picture.

• Sometimes he was the only person and right at the front.
• Sometimes he was part of a group and could be at the front, in the middle or at the back.
• Sometimes he might be in a small group but at the back.

This technique worked for Luke. Now he had a way to think about each situation he was in. He couldn't just repeat the 'good manners' that he had heard often but never really understood. By making him identify what was happening in the picture, each time there was a problem Luke was being forced to think.

What you can do if you have a child like Luke

Take your child to a place where children are playing and sit where you can watch different groups. Talk about what individual children are doing and are likely to do.

- What happens when a new child joins the group?
- What happens when one of the children has to go?
- What happens when a child from one group needs to get a ball back from another group?

Look at a picture where there are lots of people doing things. Talk about the picture.

- Who is in the picture?
- Who is important to whom in the picture?
- Why are they important to each other?
- How could the relationships change if one of the people began to do something else?

STOPPING SQUABBLES

All children fight. Most children when told to stop, will do so eventually. Other children will keep on and on niggling. Occasionally some children will turn from the person they were fighting and start fighting the person who is trying to stop them.

THE BOYS WHO BATTLED EVERYWHERE

Thomas and Joe were brothers who battled from morning 'til night. They would tip each other's things out, take each other's precious belongings and punch or kick whenever possible. There was no rest for them or their parents. When they went out they would continue the battle. In the car they would squabble nonstop. A trip around the supermarket was a misery. Visits to relatives were embarrassing.

What to do if you have warring children

If you have children behaving like Thomas and Joe, get them to make a pact about where they will and won't fight. It is pointless to tell them to stop fighting, but if you explain that it is rude to fight in public, they may be able to control when and where warfare breaks out. Knowing that they can agree, a truce will give them a strategy for declaring a war-free zone.

THE GIRL WHO WAS AT WAR WITH EVERYONE—INCLUDING HERSELF

Gemma would fall out with herself if there was no-one else in the room to fall out with. She found it easier to take offence than take a compliment. She thought life was a constant snarling match. The few friends she had she was constantly falling out with and then making up only to disagree again in a few minutes.

Gemma's parents were separated and were battling over everything; the house, the children, the car and the dog. Until these disputes were resolved, Gemma continued to fall out with everybody. Once the situation at home was sorted out, Gemma found it easier to listen. She realised people were trying to help her find ways that didn't involve fighting, to cope with her life and her friendships.

THE BOY WHO PRETENDED HIS FIGHTING WAS PLAY

Martin used his shoulders, elbows, hands, hips, knees and feet to great effect. He would nudge, push, butt, kick, punch and shove whenever he got the opportunity. If the person he was hurting protested he would give them a grin and say, 'Okay mate?', trying to pretend that what he had done had all been in good fun. It became more difficult to take Martin out because other children objected to the constant harassment. If somebody retaliated Martin would see it as unfair because, in his mind, he had turned his aggressive action into fair play.

What to do with a child like Martin
Children who are aggressive, and try to avoid being told off by saying they are only playing, have to be left in no doubt that they are in the wrong. The yardstick has to be that if someone is complaining about what they have done, then what they are doing is

THE BOY WHO COULDN'T BE TOLD

Whenever Colin did something wrong and somebody tried to sort out the problem he wouldn't listen—he would just be outraged. He would forget what had started it all off and just think that everyone was getting at him.

He would try and bully people by accusing them of being unfair, being unreasonable or hating him.

The effect on any person trying to help him was amazement, confusion and fury. His parents were exhausted because everything—even a discussion about what to watch on television turned into a, 'you don't love me', row.

How parents can avoid confrontations

It isn't unusual for parents to feel guilty and feel that they handle this sort of situation badly. Because the child makes sure the ground keeps shifting, it is essential that you stick to your point. Avoid starting sentences by saying, 'I want you to . . .'. It is much better to say, 'It is reasonable for you to . . .'. That way, if you end up in a head to head confrontation you are able to keep reminding yourself that your point is reasonable.

Make sure that when the child has done what you asked him to do, you acknowledge that he has done what he was told. Although it is easy to tell your child not to do something which irritates you, it is far more productive to tell him to **do** something which will please you.

THE FRIENDS WHO WERE NASTY TO EACH OTHER

Katy and Johanna were new friends but had no idea how to say hello to one another. When they met they would sneer at each other. They were helped when somebody suggested that they actually say, 'Hello', to each other when they met. The sneering stopped because the girls now knew how to start.

If they had only been told to stop sneering, they wouldn't have known what to do when they met. By being given something they could do, they could try it out and gain a new skill they could use in other places and with other people.

Learning how to behave peaceably is something which needs guidance and practice. Each situation requires subtle adjustments for the behaviour to be appropriate. People who behave well have been taught to behave well, even if they don't remember the teaching. Your child can be taught by you and, if you teach him well, he will learn from others when you are not there.

**People who behave well
have been taught to behave well,
even if they don't remember
the teaching.**

PART III
Effective
Parenting

Effective Parenting

Good parenting means giving children:

Concentration: clear your mind to hear what your children are saying, see what your children are doing and be aware of what is needed from you and your children will learn to clear their minds so they can hear what you are saying, see what you are doing and be aware of what is needed from them

Time: even if it is only five minutes a day. The rewards will be startling.

Recognition: delight in the children you have, don't wait for the children you thought you were going to have.

Experience: you know what the real world is. Let them know that childhood is training for adulthood and you will help them be ready for it.

Love: ask them what you do that helps them know you love them, and tell them what you need them to do so that you know they love you. Let them know that love is not finite. You have enough for many people—the more you give the more you have to give.

Respect: pay attention when they are speaking to you as if you are listening to a friend.

Interest: share your interests with them and they will share theirs with you.

Good manners: manners matter because people matter.

Self respect: teaching them how to present themselves so that other people will want to work or play with them.

Peace: a pause between activities where everyone is encouraged to be peaceful, will increase the enjoyment of life.

Reasons: whenever time, money or energy has to be spent in a particular way it is important that children are told the reason. This way they are less likely to find your behaviour unreasonable. Listen to their reasons in the way you expect them to listen to yours.

Truthfulness: is not speaking your mind. It is taking responsibility for your own actions and the consequences of them.

Explanations: the quality of the understanding will depend on the quality of the explanation.

Teaching: the best teaching happens when you let your children teach you what they need to know.

Thoughtfulness: there doesn't have to be a quick answer to everything. Some things will need thinking about before the next step is taken.

Ideas: so they can extend their world past the influence of advertisers.

Care: and teaching them what care means and how they can care for others.

Creativity: how to be their own selves, explore their own ideas and make the most of any situation rather than be overcome by disappointment when what they expected doesn't happen

Honesty: knowing how to admit to an action so that they don't fool themselves or anyone else.

Understanding: when children learn that there are many things they don't know and aren't expected to know, they will realise ignorance is the natural forerunner of the delight of learning something new.

Praise: notice achievements no matter how small.

Rest: make sure that they have enough time to sleep.

Nutrition: we are what we eat. Give food which gives them energy and strength. Notice if any foods cause them problems.

Forgiveness: teach children that mistakes are opportunities to learn for all of us.

Co-operation: work together with your children so that all of you gain satisfaction.

Discipline: children who have not learned what discipline is will not know how to use self discipline to achieve the world they want to live in

Memories: children develop memories if they know that memories are available. Talk over events of the day, discuss past holidays, birthdays, funny family events.

Acknowledgement: children need to know when something has been successful, something can work and something will be successful if they try again and improve their technique.

Flexibility: Life is full of change. Knowing that letting go of things, people or stages in life doesn't take away the memories unless you want to forget, will help children cope when they have to adjust.

This list is just a reminder. It doesn't cover everything parents can do—you are bound to have other thoughts of what any good parent will do. Effective parenting doesn't mean perfect parenting. You are not going to get it right all the time, but when you are feeling hopeful or hopeless, have a look through the list and remind yourself of what you already do and what else you can do.

**Effective parenting
doesn't mean
perfect parenting.**

Worrying

HOW TO STOP WORRYING ABOUT YOUR CHILD SO YOU
CAN START HELPING YOUR CHILD

CHILDREN WHO WORRY

WHAT CAN HAPPEN IF PARENTS WORRY AND DON'T
PAY ATTENTION TO WHAT IS NEEDED

WAYS OF HELPING YOUR CHILD DEVELOP A SENSE OF
RESPONSIBILITY

I FEEL I'M TO BLAME

WHO MAKES PARENTS WORRY?

HOW TO STOP WORRYING ABOUT YOUR CHILD SO YOU CAN START HELPING YOUR CHILD

Stop worrying—there is no point
If you can break the habit of worrying about your child you will find you will be able to help your child.

WHY DO WE WORRY?
- We feel we should.
- We think it shows we care.
- It's all we can do.
- We think because we've got it so wrong we should be worn out with worry.
- If we worry people will know we're embarrassed, we care or we're sorry.

Why some people worry
Paula worried all the time that she wasn't getting it right. She worried that she might be failing her children because she wasn't a good mother. She worried that they wouldn't have anyone to play with because people didn't like her. She worried she might feed them the wrong things and their health would suffer. She always had to be with them because she worried they might die if she wasn't. She worried if she shouted, if their clothes turned blue in the wash or if they had diarrhoea. All of these things worried her. She worried that when people noticed how much she worried they would know what a poor mother, housewife or carer she was.

Neil worried that he wasn't helping his children. He worked long hours but knew every child needed a father around to talk to. He wanted to earn as much as he could for his family but if he did that he couldn't give them time. He was stressed, his wife was stressed and the children were stressed. He worried that he wasn't as good a father to his children as his friends were to theirs.

Janet worried that because she failed at school her children might be disadvantaged. Even though she did further study she still worried that it would never be enough—that she was fundamentally stupid and could not be seen as being equal to other parents.

Sally shouted at her daughter Alice. She had had a miserable childhood, her mother had shouted at her all the time. She worried she was going to do the same to Alice. She worried that she was not equipped to give her child the proper start in life.

Jane, who had been difficult at school herself, worried that her own children would fall into the same trap. She was always worrying and needed to check constantly on how they were behaving.

Jennifer had a difficult birth. Her mother, Lisa, worried that she had been damaged by it. Lisa was unable to break the habit of worrying and Jennifer was in danger of becoming too frightened to be independent.

What can people who worry do?
Whenever we get to the point where we can stop worrying we are increasing the chance of the problem we are worrying about being solved.

THE BENEFITS OF TRAINING OURSELVES NOT TO WORRY
- We might see the solution for ourselves.
- We understand when someone else points out a solution for us.
- We can let the problem go and give ourselves a chance to enjoy the rest of life.
- We look around for solutions and may find them in unexpected places.
- We stop worrying because we realise worrying isn't necessary or helpful.
- We see new beginnings and move on instead of holding on to the past.

You can train yourself not to worry. Start by paying attention—if you can learn to pay attention to your child you will find you will know how to help him.

WHY PAY ATTENTION?
- It shows we care.
- It shows we are aware there's a problem.
- It shows our concern.
- It shows us where the solution is.

How is a parent's attention, different from a parent's worry?
When a parent is paying attention, he is leaving himself free to observe what can be done. He is looking outward rather than inward. An everyday example illustrates the point. You can sit and worry that you haven't been shopping and that there is nothing for the evening meal or, you can pay attention to what you have in the house already and see how you can put it together to make a meal.

When you are a parent you can worry that your child is not the same as everyone else's child and not look at who he is and what he can do and how you can help him.

THE BOY WHOSE PARENTS DIDN'T KNOW HIM

Josh's mother and father were anxious about him. They were always apologising to other people for him because he was so serious and sensitive. After Josh had been at school for two years the time came to enrol his younger brother, Elliot. Josh's parents were pleased to be able to tell the headteacher that their younger son was a cheerful child with a great sense of humour, unlike Josh. The headteacher looked stunned and disbelieving and said Josh had a wonderful sense of humour.

At first Josh's parents didn't believe the headteacher. They had been so busy comparing him with children who were not anxious, they had never noticed his sense of humour, let alone compared it with the sense of humour of other children. They began to listen to Josh and realised the headteacher was right. Josh did have a sense of humour. They learned their lesson and in future if either of them made a dismissive remark or said they were worried, they would be reminded by the other parent of how they had both nearly missed the enjoyment of their son's sense of fun.

If you worry you might miss something important—if you observe you will see many things. You may observe a problem or you may observe a triumph but if you are worrying you will probably observe nothing.

CHILDREN WHO WORRY

Children seem to go through times when they are easily worried. They worry they might upset the teacher, that no one will play with them in the playground or that they might be late. They could worry that their parents might die, there might be an avalanche or they might be attacked. Many children are deeply worried about how well they are doing at school. This worry might be misinterpreted by others. Children who worry, who lie awake at night in misery thinking about the next day, dreading what might or might not happen can be wrongly described as lazy, hyperactive, indifferent or suffering from a specific learning difficulty.

WHAT CAN HAPPEN IF PARENTS WORRY AND DON'T PAY ATTENTION TO WHAT IS NEEDED

THE BOY WHO WAS OVER-PROTECTED

Before Tom was born his mother had been told that he might be a very sickly child. As he grew up, she became over-protective. Any time Tom looked like he was distressed by anything, she would try to make the problem go away.

His mother's protectiveness had created a situation where Tom wasn't making progress at school. He knew, although his mum would worry, she would be protective and not get cross with him even when he didn't do what the teacher had asked.

Tom rarely did any writing at school. He would join in discussions but it seemed he could not write his ideas down. If he didn't write enough he would be kept in. But that didn't seem to bother him.

Tom may have been overwhelmed by his lack of success but he had fallen into the trap of thinking if he could avoid doing the work, somehow the whole problem would go away.

Whenever a teacher tried to help him with his reading, writing or spelling he would look at his watch, look around the room and not listen. If the teacher did manage to get him to do anything he would sigh, make silly guesses and be unable, within seconds, to remember what he had done.

When his mum tried to teach him anything at home she would prompt him quickly and urgently the minute it looked like he couldn't do it. Tom knew his mum was anxious. She was worried about his spelling, reading and writing, but her worrying could not sort these problems out. Her worrying meant that he was never given any time to think or take any responsibility to learn for himself.

Since Tom was not learning responsibility he could not benefit from teaching. He was not developing ways of learning when he was being taught.

What you need to do is teach your child how to learn.

If you only worry, you might obscure the real problem and create new problems which will distract everybody's attention. This may stop any problems being sorted out and it may mean your child never feels she has to change. You can teach your child to be responsible for her learning.

It's never too early to teach your child to be responsible.

Joanne aged one couldn't speak. When she wanted something to eat and it wasn't readily available she didn't whinge, but she let her wishes be known in an endearing way. At Easter when she was visiting her mum's friend and there were hot cross buns for a snack, she ate the piece she was offered and then toddled over to the toaster to show she wanted some more. She didn't whinge she just smiled. Her mum said Joanne had had enough and told Joanne she couldn't have anymore. Joanne looked disappointed and thought about whingeing, but she allowed herself to be distracted by being taken into the garden to look at some birds.

Learning how to distract yourself when something you want is unavailable is an important part of learning how to take responsibility for yourself. Children need to be reminded of situations where they have done well so they can use these memories to work out what to do in other situations.

Why does memory matter?
Part of taking responsibility for yourself is using your memory.

MEMORY IS DEVELOPED BY:
- Learning that there are stopping and starting places in every activity.
- Learning how to recognise the starting and stopping places in many different situations.
- Developing different routes to get from the starting position to the stopping point.

If you teach your child to be responsible you are also teaching her to use her memory. This works whether you are talking about remembering a spelling list, doing homework or bringing a letter home from school.

If you constantly compensate for your children's lack of responsibility, what you are teaching them is they don't need to use their memory unless it suits them. You then get children who are good at the things they want to be good at, but totally irresponsible about everything else.

The adults who taught children to be responsible

Helen arrived at the swimming pool for her training session and found she had forgotten her swimming costume. This was the first time she had ever forgotten her equipment but her dad insisted they go back for the costume even though the journey would mean Helen missed 45 minutes of a two-hour training session. Her dad had been planning to do something else while she was training but realised it was essential that Helen knew that forgetting didn't mean she could avoid training. Helen's dad explained that it was a nuisance for him to take her back but as her parent he knew it was his responsibility to make sure she was available for training. He didn't want her to think that because she had forgotten her costume she had found a way to get out of training. Helen had the chance to learn that it was important for her to remember everything she needed if she was taking part in an activity.

Natasha had forgotten to bring something for 'Show and Tell' at school. Her teacher's policy was if children forgot to bring something they still took a part in the activity. He realised that if children thought by forgetting to bring something to show they could avoid the task, they would be learning how to avoid responsibility. He said it was all right if she had nothing to 'show' but she would have to think of something to 'tell'. His attitude meant that Natasha could still be responsible for her part in the lesson.

Forgetting something must never be seen as a way of avoiding responsibility.

WAYS OF HELPING YOUR CHILD DEVELOP A SENSE OF RESPONSIBILITY

1. Label your child's clothes so if she leaves them somewhere she will be able to identify which are hers. She can then be responsible for her own lost property. You can't expect the person in charge of lost property to hand something over if it isn't named.
2. Make sure if your child loses something, she makes an effort to find it. Sometimes it doesn't feel worth the effort in time or energy to insist that something lost is found. You may not find it because it has been picked up by someone else but your child should know that she is responsible for her belongings. She will learn that it is better to be responsible at the time for her belongings, than spend hours afterwards looking for them.
3. Never let your child get away with pretending she didn't know the consequences when you know she did.
   • If your child misses the bus—insist she catches the next one.
   • If your child doesn't get your shopping but remembers her own—insist she goes back.
   • If your child throws a ball too hard so the person she is playing with is upset—insist she practise throwing in a way which makes the game enjoyable for others and also enjoyable for her.

Teaching your child how to remember messages

If your child forgets to give you a message, insist that she use the family noticeboard to record all messages. She needs to realise it is her responsibility to help other people fulfil their responsibilities. Give her practice in writing out messages. Explain that it is reasonable for you to give her practice because it is reasonable that she knows how to leave a message that someone else can understand.

Parents must give their children the skill of taking verbal or written messages. Without this skill children will have their potential limited, particularly when they have to write homework down, and they will drive everyone else crazy.

These days many parents think that it takes too long to teach their child to be responsible for anything and that it's quicker to do it themselves. This is a very short-term gain. A child who is not taught responsibility will lose out in the short term and in the long term. As she gets older, her parents will find they have to spend a great deal more time sorting out her problems rather than enjoying her success.

I FEEL I'M TO BLAME

Are parents to blame? Most parents are trying to make their child's life happy and successful. The way they choose to do that may be 100 per cent effective, or it may be something less than that. Sometimes the choice might have seemed effective at the time but in the long run it may have been damaging.

HOW MARTIN WAS PREVENTED FROM GETTING THE MOST OUT OF SCHOOL

Martin's mum was determined that he would arrive punctually at school and not get into trouble with the teachers. She would wake him up, wash him, stand by him while he cleaned his teeth, take out his clothes, dress him, give him delicious things to eat for breakfast and then take him to school.

Because Martin never had to make a decision or be responsible for himself he would arrive at school and wait until he was moved to the next spot. He had no idea that at school he was meant to think for himself. He knew he shouldn't be late for school but beyond that he had no idea of what was expected of him. The school thought Martin's mum would have explained it, and she thought as long as she got him to school on time the teachers would handle the rest.

How you can get your child to get the most out of school
It is important that parents give children the opportunity to learn to be responsible before they go to school. That includes making decisions, being ready to respond and anticipating what they might

have to do next. Children who start school not understanding this will be very confused. Unless the first year in school is devoted to teaching them how to learn, they may have difficulty concentrating and paying attention. Difficulty concentrating and paying attention will affect their school progress.

It is never too late to teach children how to learn, but it is essential that lack of attention and failure to learn are seen as gaps in learning and not as specific learning difficulties. Otherwise efforts directed to overcoming the problem of under-achievement may be misdirected.

THE GIRL WHO LOST OUT

Lyndsey's mum believed her child should never be unhappy or be with rough children. Whenever Lyndsey was upset she was allowed to stay home from school. Lyndsey soon developed an understanding of what to do if she wanted to stay at home. She said she was scared of crossing the playground to get into school in case she got hit by the football. So she stayed at home. She said her best friend was actually bullying her and she daren't go into school. So she stayed at home. She said she didn't understand her maths and the teacher would shout. So she didn't go into school. The school followed up all the complaints but still Lyndsey didn't go into school.

Because Lyndsey's mum felt Lyndsey should never be unhappy she didn't discuss with Lyndsey about life being full of ups and downs and everyone needing to learn to take the rough with the smooth. Because Lyndsey never went to school, no-one else could have that discussion with her either.

Children need a chance to experiment to learn

Parents who think they are protecting their children can often find they are limiting them. It is unrealistic to think you can always protect your children and unfair to think you are the only person who understands them and can help them.

THE GIRL WHO WAS CONFUSED

Gail's parents didn't feel Gail should be told that her mother was dying and only had a short time to live. Gail knew something dreadful was happening but had no-one to talk to. Her behaviour at school was dreadful. She was rude and disruptive. Although the teachers at school knew about Gail's mother they also knew that Gail was not to be told anything. This presented them with a terrible dilemma. Did they reprimand Gail when they knew she really needed support or did they ignore her behaviour and risk confusing the other pupils about what was acceptable?

Not every problem is easily solved

Some decisions have to be made taking into account one set of circumstances even if the decision will create other problems. In this case neither decision would have been problem free. The school just had to cope as sympathetically and as sensibly as they could.

PUSHY PARENTS

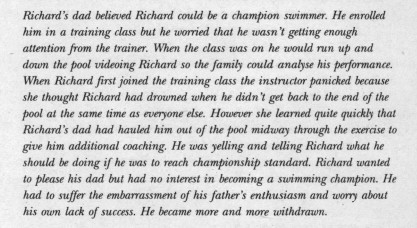

Richard's dad believed Richard could be a champion swimmer. He enrolled him in a training class but he worried that he wasn't getting enough attention from the trainer. When the class was on he would run up and down the pool videoing Richard so the family could analyse his performance. When Richard first joined the training class the instructor panicked because she thought Richard had drowned when he didn't get back to the end of the pool at the same time as everyone else. However she learned quite quickly that Richard's dad had hauled him out of the pool midway through the exercise to give him additional coaching. He was yelling and telling Richard what he should be doing if he was to reach championship standard. Richard wanted to please his dad but had no interest in becoming a swimming champion. He had to suffer the embarrassment of his father's enthusiasm and worry about his own lack of success. He became more and more withdrawn.

How to encourage your child not discourage him

Richard's mother knew that he was unhappy and had tried to discuss it with his father who had argued forcefully that he was doing the best for his son. There was nothing anyone could do to help Richard until they could help his dad.

While it is important that parents encourage their children, there is a fine line between supporting your children and overwhelming them. Be aware that other people might see the situation more realistically than you do. Weigh up other people's opinions against your own judgement.

WHO MAKES PARENTS WORRY?

It is easy to panic parents into believing that unless they are 100 per cent effective they are 100 per cent ineffective and their children may be damaged as a result. Neighbours can make parents feel uncomfortable about the way they are bringing up their children, grandparents criticise and friends question.

There are plenty of experts who frighten parents into believing their child has a problem. Parents can be made to feel unless they recognise their child as having a particular disorder, syndrome or condition they may be failing in their role as parent.

Remember how successful you have been so far as a parent and weigh up what you are being told carefully.

POINTERS FOR PARENTS TO HELP THEM STOP WORRYING

- Some children pass through the stage of being worriers but most of us still worry about things, even in adult life.
- Parents don't have to be 100 per cent effective to produce delightful, responsible citizens of the future.
- There is room for error. A mistake is an opportunity to learn.
- It is unrealistic to aim to live a perfect life.
- Parents can and should help shape their children's lives.

Does anyone have to be perfect?

Just think back over the last week. You know that you weren't 100 per cent effective. Sometimes it seemed a struggle to be 75 per cent effective. Sometimes you irritated people, sometimes your mind wasn't on the job but you will have got away with some of the mistakes.

- Not everyone who forgets to lock their car has it stolen.
- Not everyone who forgets to turn off the iron burns the house down.

• Not everyone who gets cross won't be forgiven.

How you can take yourself out of the worried state

• YOU CAN OBSERVE.

• YOU DON'T NEED TO CRITICISE.

• EVERYONE HAS THE RIGHT TO MAKE A MISTAKE.

• WE ALL LEARN AT OUR OWN PACE.

• WE ALL LEARN IN OUR OWN WAY.

• WE ALL NEED SKILLS TO UNDERSTAND HOW TO DO SOMETHING NEW.

• WE ALL NEED THE CHANCE TO PRACTISE SOMETHING WE HAVE LEARNED.

• IF YOU ARE OPTIMISTIC YOU WILL NOTICE OPPORTUNITIES.

• DON'T FORGET TO PRAISE YOURSELF OR SOMEONE ELSE FOR EFFORT.

• DON'T FORGET TO PRAISE YOURSELF OR SOMEONE ELSE FOR ACHIEVEMENT.

• NOTICE IMPROVEMENTS NO MATTER HOW SMALL.

• IF YOU LEARN TO LISTEN WITH ATTENTION YOU WILL KNOW WHAT TO DO.

Guilt

HOW TO STOP WORRYING THAT YOU ARE TO BLAME
AND START THINKING ABOUT WHAT YOU CAN DO

TAKING CONTROL

HOW TO HELP YOUR CHILD COPE WITH FRUSTRATION

THE EXERCISE

'I don't want my child to have ADD, I'm worried I might be to blame.'

ADD is an umbrella term and all children, even those who nobody would dream of describing as problem children, can show characteristics associated with ADD.

HOW TO STOP WORRYING THAT YOU ARE TO BLAME AND START THINKING ABOUT WHAT YOU CAN DO

If you are worried that your child has ADD try to become objective about what your child is doing and why it is upsetting you.

COULD IT BE:
- you get embarrassed
- you get angry and you are frightened by the way you feel
- you think other people might be upset
- you think other people might criticise you
- you worry someone might criticise your child
- you think your child is just like you, your mother, or his father's mother
- you feel dreadful because you can't stay calm
- you think your child has been spoilt by someone else
- you think you have no right to stop your child
- you are frightened by such extreme behaviour
- you want to stop it but you don't know how
- you are scared your child will damage himself
- you think it's your fault
- you've had enough and just want to get away
- you feel you have failed as a parent

TAKING CONTROL

You may feel it is impossible to gain any control over the situation but you can.

YOU CAN:
stop the anxiety by stopping criticising yourself or anyone else and trying some deep breathing. This will give you the chance to calm down, observe what is happening and stop feeling as if you are in the midst of a hurricane.

YOU CAN:
write down where and when your child causes problems and think about what else was happening at the time. Watch to see if future problems follow the same pattern.

YOU CAN:
write down things your child does which don't worry you and think what was happening then.

YOU CAN:
watch to see if you can start to predict when there may be a difficulty.

YOU CAN:
show the lists to someone else.

YOU CAN:
talk to your child about the list. This method works because by:

- listing the problems, you have a written record of what you are worried about
- listing the things that don't worry you, you are recognising that you have a child who doesn't always cause you worry
- getting other people to look at the list, you are widening your own view of your child, because other people may add items to the list you haven't thought of
- talking to your child about the list and what you are going to do will involve him in the process. He will know he is more than just a worry to you because he will see the items on the list which are not alarming you

The whole process will bring you out of the endless round of worrying and will clear your mind.

Why clearing your mind helps

By clearing your mind, you will stay in the role of observer. Remember to breathe deeply and reduce your own anxiety. Use the relaxations in the end of the book. If you use this strategy you will find that you handle the whole situation more calmly. You will be able to focus on your role as parent and supporter of your child. You will see what he needs to learn, rather than worrying about what other people think. Worrying about what other people think is a waste of time and could be damaging. It doesn't mean you don't care that your child is upsetting other people, but you won't waste your energies worrying about that. Instead all your energies can go to paying attention to what is happening, what your child still needs to learn, and what you still need to do to help.

I'm worried that it might be my fault

Have I damaged my child because:
- I try never to say no
- I hit him
- I won't let him walk to school on his own
- I try to make sure he is never bored
- I never say the teacher is right
- I sympathise with him about school
- I never put pressure on him
- I try to make him happy all the time
- I make sure he has an active life
- We have lots of family outings to museums and art galleries
- I've paid for schooling so he won't have to mix with naughty or rough children
- I won't let him go to places where people smoke
- He's an only child. I sent him to boarding school so he will always have company
- We always put our children first

Don't panic

When you have read the list, you will probably see many things that you have done, your friends have done or that were done to you as a child. None of us lives in a perfect world. Some decisions we make are not the best decisions but they are carefully thought about at the time. If you are panicking, comfort yourself by thinking of your own childhood. Think of some things your parents did for you.

- Took you to the dentist.
- Made you tidy your room.
- Bought you some sensible shoes.
- Taught you to swim.
- Allowed you to eat sweets.
- Banned you from watching television.
- Shouted at you when they were angry.
- Stopped you doing things you wanted when you had upset them.
- Made you wear a coat.
- Banned you from seeing your girlfriend.
- Let you choose whether you went to school or not.

Some of these decisions were helpful and some were unhelpful. Some you raged against at the time and now you see the point. Some you are determined you will never do to your own child. Parents can't help making decisions that their children think are unfair, silly or mean.

Children can learn how to manage their disappointment, disillusionment or distress at decisions their parents make.

HOW TO HELP YOUR CHILD COPE WITH FRUSTRATION

David was volatile. If a decision was made he didn't like or he was asked to do something he didn't want to, whether at school or home, he would explode with rage. If the rage happened at school, David would hit other children, verbally defy teachers and on one occasion pushed a teacher out of the way. If the rage happened at home, David would break things, hurt his sisters and swear at everyone.

David's parents heard about an exercise which could diffuse rage. They talked to David and told him about the exercise. They suggested all three of them practise the exercise so that next time he felt rage, they would all know what to do. They explained that the exercise helped reduce the tension that was causing the rage. If it worked all the energy that was going into the rage would go into thinking through the problem that had caused his frustration in the first place and had led to the rage.

THE EXERCISE

The Hug
Wrap both arms tightly around your body—give yourself a big hug.

The Stretch
Now stretch your arms out straight in front. Bring your arms round at shoulder level so they are stretched out to your sides. Let your arms go down and clasp your hands behind your back. Finally lift your clasped hands as high as you can behind you.

Go back to the hug and repeat five times.

Make sure at every point you are stretching as hard as you can.

For any family who is experiencing difficulties this exercise done in the morning will reduce the number of times stressful situations will arise. In David's case it was instantly successful. David no longer needed to explode because now he knew that he had an option. He didn't overcome all of the problems immediately but he was no longer violent or physically destructive.

Why such a simple exercise works
It probably sounds ridiculous that something which is a 'warm-up' exercise for physical education could have such a profound effect. Even if, when you try it, your child looks murderous and flops his arms around making you feel like giving up, crying or running screaming from the room, the mere fact that you are doing the exercise will reduce the tension.

You will both end up smiling at each other. You will find you have more intellectual energy because you're not being drained by your emotions. If your child's emotional level is reduced he will have more intellectual energy and together you will have double the energy to work out your problems.

My child has terrible problems. He can't be helped that easily

If you really believe your child has such terrible problems he can't be helped, think about what has happened in his life so far.

HE MIGHT BE HAVING DIFFICULTIES BECAUSE:
- he had a difficult birth
- he's got allergies
- he's adopted
- he was very ill when he was a baby
- he can't sleep
- he's a picky eater
- he's younger than everybody else in the class.

All of these difficulties can cause problematic behaviour. All the problematic behaviour can be overcome.

Why would a difficult birth lead to problematic behaviour?

The fact that a child had a difficult birth may be the reason for his behaviour, but it does not mean that he will always have to misbehave. You can understand what has caused the behaviour and help a child who had a difficult birth or other early childhood trauma learn how to cope.

The consequences of a difficult birth

A child who experienced a difficult birth could be having difficulties in later life because:

- he has already had to fight very hard to survive
- his mother may have been traumatised by the birth
- the whole family may have been exhausted by the worry
- his mother may have felt responsible for the difficulty of the birth
- his mother may have taken a long time to build a relationship with the baby
- his mother may not have been given the nurturing she needed after the baby's birth

• he may be the only member of his family to have experienced the trauma of a difficult birth

Ways you can tell if your child's behaviour is due to a difficult birth.

1. He may feel very insecure. He may have trouble with new experiences and find them alarming or frightening.
2. He may find making a choice difficult. Typically, if offered a choice of flavours of ice creams he will find making a decision agonising and may not be able to do it.
3. He may find sustaining interest in playing with other children difficult. He may invite children home but another brother or sister will end up playing with the visitor. He will have wandered off and 'done his own thing'.
4. He may have had difficulty sleeping in the early years.
5. He may have difficulty asserting himself. This may not be obvious to other people but the child has confided in you.
6. He is unexpectedly interested in people. He may not seem to be bothered about other people and then surprise you with his insight into someone else's problem.

Ways to help your child achieve his potential despite the fact he had a difficult birth

When Alistair's mother dropped him off somewhere to play, or to do an after schools activity, Alistair would ask whether she was picking him up. If his mother said she wasn't sure—meaning if it wasn't going to be her it would be Alistair's father or grandmother—Alistair felt abandoned.

If you have a child like Alistair, explain to him that finding new experiences alarming is a result of his difficult birth. He can learn to have a different reaction based on his experiences since he was born. You can remind him of the new experiences he has had and survived. If he is uncertain about a new experience you can suggest he does the new thing to make you happy. Explain to him you know he is going to meet new experiences all his life and you want to teach him how to deal with them successfully.

A difficult birth, like other childhood traumas, can create a child who is so frightened something else might go wrong that he uses all his attention to check and see where the next problems might be. As a result he will make progress more slowly than he needs to until the problem is sorted out.

An insecure child needs to know what is going on in his family. He is not sure that when people go away they are going to come back. He can easily feel abandoned and bereft. You can teach him to recognise that his insecurity isn't real, even though it might be triggered when something unexpected happens. Use the relaxations.

**Focus your energies on
what your child needs to learn
and what you can do to
help your child learn.**

Fear

'Maybe your child is too frightened to pay attention?'
Children who have missed the chance to feel secure will need
special help to cope with the feelings that insecurity produces.

IF CHILDREN HAVE MISSED OUT ON:
- time with the family
- company of others
- explanations for what is happening at school
- answers to questions
- friends
- being able to say how they feel
- the chance to be a baby
- the chance to be a child
- the chance to feel secure

If there has been family trauma, at some point the children will
need support to understand how they have been affected and how
they can move on.

You can help your child

- FEEL SAFE
- HANDLE NEW EXPERIENCES
- COPE WITH STRESS
- ACCEPT THE UNPREDICTABILITY OF LIFE

What every child needs is an explanation for why it is reasonable
to feel insecure. It is important to explain that life isn't predictable.
Although we try to plan for things to go well each day, there are
always things that go wrong or happen differently from the way they
were planned.

It is natural for children who have suffered a trauma where they
felt powerless, to want life to be predictable. However it is important
for parents and children to recognise that not every eventuality can

be planned for. Most children want to have a structure because it makes them feel comfortable. Children who have suffered a trauma need a structure so they can feel safe.

HOW TO HELP YOUR CHILD COPE WITH THE UNEXPECTED

Talk to your child about the day's events which haven't happened in the expected way. Talk about what happened instead. That way your child will begin to realise that:

- planning doesn't result in protection
- unexpected events do not have to lead to disaster

An insecure child wants everything to be fair and everyone to behave with kindness. Obviously no-one can guarantee this or ensure that it happens.

Explaining that life isn't always fair
Explain to your child that within the family, parents might be able to be fair and kind but in the outside world they have very little control. Parents can control some things.

PARENTS CAN CONTROL:
- when the television goes on
- bedtime
- what is bought at the shops
- where to go on holiday
- how much pocket money children get

Or can they?

PARENTS CAN'T CONTROL:
- their children's friends at school
- how teachers teach
- what their children will be interested in
- bullies
- what their children eat away from home

Even if they'd like to!

TEACHING YOUR CHILD ABOUT CONTROL

Children often enjoy control because they see control as providing fairness. Remind your child of times when she needs you to be firm—and when she doesn't. For instance, when she is playing with another child at home and they have an argument she may want you to be firm or she may want to sort it out for herself.

What everyone has to keep learning is that life is not smooth, and in order to live life to the full you have to learn how you can best deal with the unexpected, the unwelcome or the unpleasant. Sometimes you may deal with a problem yourself, sometimes you may talk it over with your family or friends and sometimes you may go for expert help.

If your child is sensitive you will want to protect her but you have to use your judgement about when and how to interfere.

HOW TO HELP YOUR CHILD COPE WITH BEING SENSITIVE

If you are worried about your child's teacher because he shouts and you know your child hates it if people shout, you have several positive options, any of which you could use.

YOU CAN:
- talk to the headteacher
- remove the child from the school
- talk to the child about how she can cope in the classroom
- do some background work at home so your child feels confident she knows what to do in the lessons—it could be how to cope with somebody shouting or it could be extra maths
- teach your child to relax

Why children need to learn to cope
Remember your aim as a parent is to prepare your child for being an adult. Even sensitive children are going to be adults.

ADULTS NEED TO:
- be able to cope with stress
- be independent
- be responsible for themselves
- care for others
- understand their role as part of a community

Whenever you try to help your child, it is important you think about what she is going to learn as a result of your efforts. If she is going to learn that you will take up the cudgels and defend her no matter what, she will never have to learn how to deal with a difficult situation. You can only keep protecting a child in this way until she is sixteen. Even before sixteen you take a risk that if you keep protecting your child you will prevent her from learning sufficient life skills. If you haven't taught her to be responsible for herself while you could protect her, at sixteen she will stand alone and defenceless. In the end you may lose any influence over your own child. You can't protect her forever. The earlier a child learns the importance of self discipline and reasonable behaviour the better.

HOW TO HELP YOUR CHILD COPE WITH CHANGE

Some sensitive children find it hard to accept change. This may have to do with the difficulties they have experienced. When change is about to happen, and it does happen for everybody, your child has a number of possibilities.

YOUR CHILD CAN:
- refuse to acknowledge it is happening
- resist
- refuse to change
- cry
- complain bitterly
- stand on the side lines, watching until he feels he has enough information to know how to join in
- swoop into the activity without a backward glance causing havoc by dominating or disrupting
- move in to the activity confidently, taking account of what is happening and add to everyone's enjoyment by his presence

WONDERMENT—AN ANTIDOTE TO FEAR

If you can teach your child to wonder, you can teach her to enjoy change. You can develop in your child the skill of wonderment. You may think that wonderment is something you are born with and this could be true, but for some people wonderment fades. Wonderment can be taught. When it is taught your child's horizons will widen beyond belief.

THE BOY WHO HAD NEVER REALISED HE COULD WONDER AT ALL

Paul was terrified of stepping into the outside world. Although he was nearly fifteen he never travelled anywhere by public transport and would insist that his parents take him everywhere. If they couldn't take him but instead provided him with a taxi he felt hard done by and panicked. For Paul everything that didn't involve his parents or his home was a blank. He would panic and refuse to take any risk. In Paul's mind any change involved unacceptable risks. He would not wonder which taxi company would come, how long his journey would take or which way the taxi driver would choose to go. Instead he would panic because he couldn't take responsibility and life seemed too unpredictable.

Lydia was a child like Paul.

HOW LYDIA WAS TAUGHT TO WONDER STEP-BY-STEP

Whenever there was a new situation Lydia panicked. Lydia was invited to join the orchestra because she was coming on so well with the violin. When she found out that orchestra practice was held at another school on a Saturday morning her delight vanished and her terror took over. Lydia's parents arranged for Lydia's grandad to drop her off at the school. This was the first time they had ever let anyone else take Lydia to an event. Up until this time Lydia had been taken everywhere by her mother. Because it was a Saturday and Lydia's mother worked, there was no alternative and grandad was quite pleased to be involved in Lydia's music. Lydia's grandad knew that she always panicked whenever things were new for her. He knew that if he wasn't careful he would be taking Lydia back home without her ever having entered the rehearsal room.

Lydia's grandad had a plan. He knew if he could get Lydia to be interested in the detail of the rehearsal, her fear would be overcome. As he drove he began to think out loud about the practice.

- Sometimes he thought out loud about things he knew were wrong, and he hoped Lydia would feel she had to correct him.
- Sometimes he thought out loud about things that Lydia could check on once she got to the rehearsal.
- Sometimes he thought out loud about things Lydia could easily tell him because she already knew the answers.

He was very careful not to think out loud about things that might worry Lydia. Lydia was the sort of person who, the minute she thought there was something she felt she had made a mistake about, would use that as a justification for not continuing with the activity.

What Lydia's grandad wondered

'I wonder if your headteacher will be in charge of the orchestra?'

Lydia put her grandad right, as he knew she would, and explained it was going to be run by the music teacher.

'I don't suppose the percussion section are part of the orchestra.'

Lydia explained that they were in the orchestra and they would be there, too.'

'I suppose it will only be children from your school there.'

Lydia said that there would be children from other schools.

If Lydia was at a co-education school her granddad might have wondered aloud about whether there were any boys in the orchestra. Knowing Lydia was not keen on boys, it would be better if he did not wonder about this. Other things he chose not to wonder about were whether there would be a break, who she would sit next to and what time it finished. He left out anything that Lydia could have turned into a worry.

Things Lydia needed to know

Because he knew Lydia might panic, her grandad made sure she knew certain details were clear.

- He would be there to pick her up at the end.

- He would get out of his car and wait by the gate.
- He would be fascinated to hear all about what it had been like.

Why Grandad made the plan

Grandad made the plan because he knew Lydia had to think about what she was going to do, so she could stop thinking about herself. If you have a child like Lydia it is better if everyone is interested in the **event** rather than in the child's **individual performance** or the **child's fears**. Then the child will see the event as an activity full of interest and possibilities and will look outward. This is better than the child focusing on herself, her fears and her own performance and thus restricting her view of what else is happening.

How to keep a child's view broad

Some of the questions which Grandad used to keep Lydia's view broad were:

- I wonder how many other children will be there?
- I wonder if you sit down or stand up?
- I wonder if it's in the gym or the hall?
- I wonder whether teachers from other schools go?
- I wonder how old the oldest person who goes is?
- I wonder who the youngest person in the orchestra is?

By the time they got to the orchestra practice, Lydia had moved through her panic and into the world of the practice. Her grandad had given her the chance to rehearse the event with someone she trusted, but it had been done in such a pleasant way that she was calmly and eagerly anticipating the rest of the morning.

When Lydia came out of the rehearsal her grandad was where he had said he would be. On the journey home Lydia told him about the practice. Lydia had enjoyed herself and so she chatted quite easily for about five minutes. Then, when she was quiet, her grandad asked her a few more questions.

You too can extend your child's appreciation of an event and also find out if she needs some adult support to gain more from it in the future. By extending the discussion after your child has told you her first impressions, she will get far more benefit from what she has done.

Lydia's report to her grandad

Lydia told her grandad about the boy she sat next to and the conductor. She described what the conductor was wearing. Lydia explained that they had played a piece she knew well. She told her grandad that when you are in an orchestra you have to be quiet when the conductor bangs his stick on his music stand.

Lydia's grandad asked if there had been a break. Lydia told him there had been a short break. The girl who sat in front of Lydia had shared her snack with her and then had shown Lydia where the toilets were. Lydia and her grandad talked about what Lydia could take as a snack the next week.

Did the plan work?

In Lydia's case it did. If, however, the next week Lydia's grandad had got a call saying Lydia felt too frightened to go, he would have had the confidence to say he would go and get her. He realised it might take a little time for her to get over the habit of resisting anything new, but she had had such a lovely time last rehearsal that he knew it was right to keep encouraging her by insisting she should go.

HOW TO HELP A FRIGHTENED CHILD CONQUER FEAR AND CONQUER THE WORLD

Jack was swearing and shouting and slamming doors because he couldn't cope with some of the work at school.

All the pupils in Jack's class had to do a geography survey. They were supposed to do the survey in a town 10 kilometres from school. Jack hated anything unpredictable where he would have to cope with something new. Jack was terrified, and his parents went to see the teacher. Jack's parents asked whether the work was essential and found that it was a requirement of the course. Jack's teacher decided to give him the opportunity to do some work near where Jack lived. He would only have to go as far as half a kilometre in any direction from his own home.

The survey was to look at the types of housing, transport and shopping available in the area. Jack could also look at other forms of land use—parks, playgrounds, schools and industry.

Jack still was resistant to the instructions because he felt incapable of undertaking the project. He still felt he didn't have the ability to work outside the protection of his home or school. The wide world was frightening to Jack. It could be unpredictable and he wasn't sure he understood the rules.

Jack's teacher used a similar tactic to Lydia's grandad.

How questions helped overcome Jack's fear
Jack's teacher sat and chatted with him and in the course of the conversation wrote down the following questions about the area around Jack's house:

- Are there any roads with schools on them?
- Are there more than two bus routes?
- Are there any bus stops on the main road?
- Are there more than four roads which have buses which travel along them?
- Are there any empty shops and what businesses were in them last?
- Are there more than ten houses up for sale?

Using this format Jack and his teacher devised fourteen more questions. The only skills Jack needed to be able to answer these were labelling the page clearly so he would not get muddled up and making a tally chart of the information he had collected.

By limiting the expectations placed on Jack it was possible to see where the successes and failures were occurring. Jack was enthusiastic to begin with. Jack found some data easy to collect and some stressful. He was able to identify why some things were hard. One difficulty occurred when he was counting houses for sale. He had been chased by a dog when he was much younger and had avoided that particular street ever since. Jack told his parents and they discussed various options:

- Jack could leave that part of the question
- Jack's dad could walk down the street with him
- Jack's dad could wait halfway down the street in the car
- Jack's dad could wait at the top of the street
- Jack's dad could wait at work by the telephone and Jack carry the money to make a telephone call
- Jack could ring his dad at the end of the survey of that street

- Jack could see the street as just like any other street and not need his parent's involvement at all

After talking over the options it was decided his father would wait at the top of the street while Jack collected the information.
  By discussing options:

- Jack's parents kept a parenting role but still left Jack to make decisions.
- Jack was encouraged to recognise the steps necessary to achieve independence.
- Jack was supported in his decision about the stage he had reached.

How Jack's parents might have created a false impression of the real world

Jack's parents might have chosen an option which would not have allowed Jack to develop. They could have made excuses:

- The work's too difficult and it's unreasonable to expect Jack to do it.
- We've both got jobs and we've no time to be doing this with Jack.
- We send him to school to be taught—the teachers are paid to sort out the problems.
- Everyone knows Jack has a problem—he shouldn't be asked to do something so difficult.
- Jack has special needs so if the teachers at school want him to do the work they need to provide someone to go with him.
- Jack's older brother is home from university so we'll get him to do it for Jack.
- Jack can stay off on the day the work has to be handed in.
- Jack's cold is too bad for him to be out on the streets.
- Jack did all the work but he's lost it.
- Jack didn't understand the question.
- Jack would have done it but we have had a lot of problems in the family.
- Jack didn't want to do it so we told him it was up to him.
- Jack was bored by it.
- Jack doesn't like geography.

All these options create a false impression in children. They begin to believe they will always be able to get out of any situation that doesn't make them feel completely comfortable.

Why the option Jack's parents took was best

As adults we know a childhood, supported by parents who realise their role is to train their child, is the best preparation you can have for adult life.

> You can give a fearful child
> options that will help him
> conquer his fear—and conquer the world.

Teaching recklesss children

THE CONSEQUENCES OF ACTION

TEACHING RECKLESS CHILDREN HOW TO BEHAVE

TEACHING RECKLESS CHILDREN WHY WE HAVE RULES

TEACHING RECKLESS CHILDREN HOW TO BEHAVE IN THE
CLASSROOM

WHY DO SOME PEOPLE NEED TO BE TAUGHT

CONSEQUENCES

THE CONSEQUENCES OF ACTION

- Every action has a consequence.
- Some consequences are positive.
- Some consequences are negative.
- Some consequences can be negative or positive depending on how they affect different individuals.
- Every parent must think about consequences.
- Every child must be taught about consequences.
- Successful living comes from thinking about consequences before acting.
- Successful learning is produced by developing thinking.
- The more expert your thinking before you act the more likely your chances for success.

Reckless children rarely understand the consequences of action.

CRAIG WAS RECKLESS BECAUSE HE DIDN'T UNDERSTAND

Craig was confused by what was expected of him and didn't understand the consequences of his actions. His school used a method of assertive discipline. If a child misbehaved in class the teacher wrote the child's name on the board. If the child was silly again the teacher put a tick by the name. Three ticks in one lesson meant a detention. Most children in the school understood the system and few received even two ticks. Craig's behaviour had been getting worse for two weeks. He was put on detention for his silliness in class. At the detention Craig behaved like the 'tough lads' who were in the detention with him. The teachers were annoyed. They had been prepared to try to help Craig overcome his silliness, but Craig seemed happy to ignore the seriousness of what he was doing and carried on being rude and difficult in the detention.

Craig didn't understand where his behaviour was leading him. He didn't understand that his behaviour would lead to consequences that he might not like. Craig's mother was called to the school to discuss Craig's behaviour. Craig hadn't learned strategies to stop a downward spiral in his own behaviour. Instead, he copied children around him. Craig was not unusual in this. Children copy other children they notice. They notice other children's poor behaviour because poor behaviour is noticeable.

If a child doesn't understand that the purpose of a detention or any other punishment is to help him understand the ethic of the school, he will make up his own reason for why he received the punishment. In Craig's case he decided he was on detention because he was naughty. He looked at how others were behaving in the detention room and decided that was how naughty children behaved when on a detention—so he copied them.

Before he entered the detention room the important thing for Craig to know was what the teacher's expectations would be for how he should behave. He should have been told he would be expected to show that he knew how to work in class the way the school wanted him to. When Craig didn't behave, because no-one explained their expectations to him, the teacher thought Craig was incapable of behaving well even when he was being given a sanction that very few other children in the school ever needed.

Craig's mother realised what had happened when she spoke to Craig. She recognised his confusion and talked to Craig about how each situation in life has its own rules. She explained that people often assume that everyone knows the rules, so to be successful he would have to learn how to check out each new situation. Checking was an important skill for Craig to develop.

The invaluable thing Craig learnt from this detention was that there are consequences which follow from every action. His mother sat down with him and discussed consequences. She explained that:

- some consequences are good and some are bad
- some consequences happen quickly—a merit award for good work or a detention for some misdemeanour
- some consequences are much harder to spot

Not every consequence happens quickly

Craig's mother explained to him that every uncooperative action of a child may not be punished immediately but when the child wants to do something out of the ordinary he may not be allowed. She reminded him of the time his sister, Christine, had been irritating all day. When she asked if she could stay up to watch a television program her mother said no.

Craig's mother also pointed out that each cooperative action of a child may not be praised but when he needs something out of the ordinary it can happen. They remembered when Craig's brother, Ben, had been helpful all week. When he missed the bus for football practice his mum ran him to the sports ground in the car. Usually she would have let him wait for the next bus.

The first thing that children have to understand is that in the normal course of their lives they are expected to be responsible. This means thinking about what is expected in new situations and checking whether they are right by observation or by asking other people who seem to know what they are doing.

TEACHING RECKLESS CHILDREN HOW TO BEHAVE

1. Ask your children to tell you where they find it easiest to behave. You could make some suggestions—beach, swimming pool, cricket training, gymnastics class. Write down the answer.
2. Ask them why they find it easy.
3. Ask them how they decide what to do.

Children seem to make decisions as to how they will behave on the basis of:

- what they assume is correct behaviour
- what they have got away with before
- not wanting to be told off
- thinking they can get away with it
- thinking, even if they get into trouble, it's worth it for the 'kicks'

Fourteen year old Jenny thought that because she had paid for her ticket she was entitled to have as much fun as she could and that she needn't worry about the swimming pool rules.

Her brother Barry knew what the rules were and knew he should abide by them but always seemed to escape trouble. He was one of life's 'invisibles'.

Katy always behaved perfectly at the swimming pool. She would be very upset if the pool attendant had to tell her off. For Katy getting told off was mortifying.

Edward, Jonathan and Justine had all worked out if they were polite and made sure the pool attendant had noticed them when they were being good, they would be able to get away with breaking a few rules.

Elliot loved to live his life 'on the edge' and having the whistle blown at him, by the pool attendant, just confirmed he was taking a risk. He would bounce on to the next activity unaffected by any telling off he had received.

The behaviour of these children is manageable if there is someone else taking control. Even Elliot will be protected because the pool attendant might tell him to get out for his own safety.

Katy, Edward, Elliot and Justine were asked how they would behave if the lifeguard had to deal with an emergency on the other side of the pool. They were very excited at the idea of being in a swimming pool with no restrictions. Their responses were:

- I'd run up and down the side of the pool pushing people in
- I'd dive into the shallow end
- I'd push people off the diving board
- I'd play with the life belts
- I'd splash other people
- I'd turn on the hose
- I'd dive under the water and grab people's legs
- I'd swim in the baby pool

The children then discussed the consequences of each of their actions. People might get hurt. They might skid on the side. It suddenly dawned on them all that people might get hurt because of what they were doing. They understood why the rules were there.

All children need to understand why rules are made and the consequences of breaking any rule.

TEACHING RECKLESS CHILDREN WHY WE HAVE RULES

List with your children times that they can take responsibility, even though no-one tells them to and no-one supervises them.

1. Feeding pets.
2. Cleaning teeth.
3. Crossing the road carefully.
4. Putting litter in the bin.
5. Not throwing sand or stones.
6. Carrying plates to the kitchen.
7. Making a cup of tea.
8. Putting shoes on.
9. Being ready for school on time.
10. Packing their own bags for school.

Go on to list why they should take responsibility for those things on the list.

1. If they feed their pets, the animals will be healthy and well cared for.
2. If they clean their teeth, they can still eat sweets and their teeth will last longer.
3. If they cross the road carefully, they will have more chance of staying alive.
4. If they put litter in the bin, they can have the enjoyment of living in clean spaces.
5. If they don't throw things, they won't endanger others.
6. If they carry plates to the kitchen or make a cup of tea they are being helpful.
7. If they get themselves ready for school or going out, it makes life more efficient and easier for everyone.

TEACHING RECKLESS CHILDREN HOW TO BEHAVE IN THE CLASSROOM

Having established that your children can take responsibility for themselves at home, the next question to ask, if you are concerned about behaviour at school is; 'What should you take responsibility for in the classroom?' Write down ideas such as not talking, getting on with work and not messing about. Next write down what the consequences are, in school, if a child does not take responsibility.

1. Being given a detention.
2. Being told off.

3. Having to write lines.
4. Having to work in the headteacher's office.

Discuss with your children why teachers use sanctions like those on your list. Make a list of what children can do to show that they understand how to behave when they have done something wrong such as at a detention.

1. Go into the room quietly.
2. Listen to what you have to do.
3. Do not let anyone else distract you.
4. Get on with your work.
5. If you are unsure about what you have to do, ask in a polite way for some help.
6. If other children are messing about—in Craig's case two boys behind him had been pushing him—then ask the teacher if you can move.
7. Think about the best way to ask the teacher questions so it appears you are being cooperative rather than disruptive.

Every child needs to understand that how they speak to another person will have a direct consequence on what happens next. Children who speak politely, show that they are wanting to work with the teacher and not against him, will get better teaching. The teacher will be able to use his energy to explain what is needed rather than using his energy to cope with rudeness and lack of cooperation.

Teaching reckless children how to ask a teacher a question politely

Remind your child that the teacher is a human being and will appreciate being treated as one. To ask the teacher a question politely your child needs to:

- check whether he needs to put up his hand or go out to where the teacher is and ask the teacher quietly
- choose a tone of voice that is not whingeing or bullying but is audible and open to the teacher's help
- move the chair quietly—practise this at home
- walk out to the teacher in a non-provocative way
- speak politely

Give your child opportunities to practise at home

If you are aware your child scowls, looks sullen or has a silly grin on his face when he feels under pressure, encourage him to practise asking questions in front of a mirror so he can see what happens to his face. Explain to him what is happening and that the expression on his face will have an immediate effect on the teacher even before he makes his request. Ask him to select an expression he thinks he will be able to use without upsetting the teacher. Sometimes you will have to suggest actual sentences your children can use when they are speaking to their teachers. Some children need your help to take the next step.

THE TALE OF THE BOY WHO DIDN'T KNOW
HOW TO SPEAK TO THE TEACHER

Pat was having trouble with his sums and used all sorts of delaying tactics. When the teacher noticed he wasn't doing any maths Pat was on the defensive. When she suggested he start with the easy sums, he got angry and said he could do them and put down his pen. He had created a stalemate situation. When he talked to his mother about what had happened they thought of several other sentences Pat could have used instead.

He could have

- asked why he needed to do them
- asked how many he needed to do before he went on to the next ones
- done some without question and then asked

THE TALE OF THE BOY WHO DID KNOW
HOW TO SPEAK TO A TEACHER

Mark was having difficulty with his maths and asked his teacher for help. He was confused when the teacher suggested he start with some easy sums. He said it wasn't the easy ones he was having trouble with. However, Mark stayed polite and the teacher explained that if he started with the easy ones she would have more idea of how to help him when he got to the harder ones. Mark did as he was asked and, to his surprise, found the teacher was right.

THE BOY WHO WAS RECKLESS AND IMPULSIVE

James was angry anytime anyone asked him to do anything he didn't want to do. He didn't understand the consequences of his action in the long term. A teacher came into James' classroom and asked him to join a group doing specific work on writing. James had known before that he should be at the writing workshop but he thumped out of the room disrupting the lesson. He shuffled along complaining the whole time that he'd been withdrawn from a lesson. James was unable to stop his complaining and each new complaint he thought of made him feel angrier. By the time he got to the room where the writing workshop was happening he was completely uncooperative. The other pupils were working with enjoyment but James ruined the experience for himself. James' behaviour led the teacher to ask him to sit at a table on his own. James took this as a reason to be outraged because he felt picked on. Why should he have to sit somewhere different? James felt the teacher was deliberately making him angrier. He had no idea his original crossness and his refusal to join in was destroying an enjoyable and important workshop for the others. When James got home he complained long and loud to his mother. Life was unfair, school was unfair and she should go up to the school and sort out the teacher. John raged around the house slamming doors and arguing with everyone in sight. When he finally went quiet he was found cutting up his new school jumper.

How had James become so reckless?

James was used to people taking responsibility for his problems. From a very early age his parents had looked for support. First it was the health visitor, then the family doctor, then the social worker, the psychologist and finally the paediatrician. James was one of those people who went round and round the system. He had a file which documented everyone's professional response to 'the problem of James'.

James and the basketball team

James could take responsibility for his own actions. He joined a basketball team. He found out at the first session he wasn't as fit as the others. James worked on his fitness until he could keep up with the others in the team. Whenever he was going to basketball he made his breakfast, packed his bag, wore the right clothes, arrived on time, got home on time and got changed once he got home. He had never done this before. He could have added being unfit to the catalogue of problems he had but he chose not to. James saw being unfit as his own problem which he could do something about. He wanted to be in the team so he made sure he got there.

James at school and home
When it didn't suit James to take responsibility for his own actions at school and at home he got angry. Once he became angry, he was taken out of the situation he was disrupting and the responsibility to sort out his behaviour was given to someone else.

Why did James behave like this?
James often thought he had won. He no longer had to do what he disliked and he could watch and wait while other people tried to come up with alternatives. For lots of children the consequence of being removed from a lesson because of their bad behaviour is feeling embarrassed or mortified. For James the consequence of being removed from a lesson was often a feeling of success.

Why James kept getting angry
James showed anger —> consequence —> removed from the lesson —> consequence —> James felt successful —> consequence —> James continued to show anger when he was asked to do something he decided he didn't want to do.

Every time the cycle was repeated James felt he had handled the situation successfully. He felt justified in getting angry again when he didn't want to do something.

What James was losing
This cycle only seems successful to an immature person. There were long-term consequences.

- James missed out on learning the skills for adulthood.
- James did not progress socially because he was not part of his peer group as they learned to cope with things that were new or difficult.
- James was tense all the time because he kept himself in readiness to explode.

- James was not learning a range of emotions to deal successfully with conflict.
- James was missing out on large parts of his school education.
- James believed his problems were somebody else's responsibility to sort out.
- James was not gaining an understanding of how any organisation (such as school) works.
- James was not gaining an understanding of how his behaviour affects others or himself.

The earlier you can start to teach consequences the better. Someone like James has learned that the consequences of his behaviour will always be someone else's responsibility if it doesn't suit him to take responsibility himself.

Why it is essential to teach consequences to a child like James.

1. James needs to learn that education is a chance to build up skills, information and experience. It should not be a series of missed opportunities. If the opportunities are missed, for whatever reason, it is the responsibility of society through its schools to offer the chance to make up for lost opportunities. It is the student's responsibility to take that chance.

2. James needs to know there are consequences every time he does something. The consequences may be positive or negative depending on what his behaviour has been like. He may think the consequences of his behaviour are positive because he has got what he has wanted. In reality the consequences for James are negative because he is not making progress and the school will have to find some other solution for him.

3. The role of the school is to teach children. Misbehaviour is a signal to teachers that children have not yet learned how to behave in school. There is a limit to how much time can be devoted to James without endangering other pupils' rights to the teacher's time and energy.

4. If James can't behave he may find himself being asked to leave one school and move to another. If he doesn't learn to behave there he will be reducing his chances still further.

BEN WRECKED EVERYTHING

Ben would 'mess about' in the morning and everybody would be late. He was rude and nasty to all the members of his family. He never helped tidy up and just messed up any room he happened to be in. He would go into his brother's room without asking and wreck his brother's possessions.

Family life was miserable.

How to teach consequences to a child like Ben

1. Every time Ben is late and delays everyone else, he loses time doing something he wants to do.

2. Every time Ben is rude and nasty, he loses ten minutes of something he wants to do.

3. Every time Ben doesn't help get the meal, he doesn't have a dessert.

4. Every time Ben messes up a room, he can't have free time until it has been tidied.

5. Every time Ben damages a possession, something of his is confiscated until he has found a way of replacing or repairing the broken item.

A consistent approach to a child like Ben, constantly emphasising there are consequences, will show him that it is worth thinking before he acts. Family conversations about situations and the consequences that have happened to all family members will help Ben realise consequences can be good and bad. If Ben begins to tidy his room, be on time etc. the reward should be the opposite of the sanction, such as five minutes extra free time, having dessert and not losing a treasured item.

Do not give a child a special treat for behaving the way you would expect any person to behave.

WHY DO SOME PEOPLE NEED TO BE TAUGHT CONSEQUENCES?

Many people can't remember anyone having to teach them consequences—so surely there must be something wrong with children who don't understand that there are consequences?

Before everybody had cars, anyone who had to catch a bus to school realised the consequence of not being ready on time.

Before twenty-four hour shopping, anyone who hadn't been to the shop by five o'clock knew they would have to make a different meal, go without new socks for the next day or put up with the headache because they had run out of aspirin.

Before microwave ovens, anyone who forgot to peel the potatoes would have to delay the meal for another half hour until the potatoes were ready.

With technological changes, children haven't needed to learn the consequences of their actions in the same way as children did even in the recent past. Vacuum cleaners, dishwashers, microwaves, cars, credit cards, computers and twenty-four hour shopping have all taken away children's opportunities to learn that their actions will have consequences.

Children today must be given the chance to experience and learn that their actions will have consequences.

Children can be taught about consequences if the adults responsible for them think about why the child hasn't learned, rather than thinking the child can't learn.

There is always a consequence, and all of us have to be aware of how to produce the most positive consequences from every one of our actions.

Children will believe that their behaviour has no consequences, if we choose to do nothing when they misbehave.

Children who understand the consequences of their behaviour and choose to behave thoughtfully, will enhance their own prospects and the quality of life of other people.

Solving the problem

HOW TO FIND A SOLUTION

Now you know why your child has a problem what do you do next?

You have to be very careful about the next step. You know your child is having difficulties and you may decide you want expert help. Be clear what you want is what you get. You have to decide whether you want a reason and a solution or do you want a reason and special consideration.

Points to think about
- Is it your child's behaviour that is a problem?
- Do you want a solution to the problem?
- Is your child's behaviour because of the problem?
- Do you want special consideration to be given to your child because of the problem?

You need to decide whether you want your child to be seen as an individual with a problem that needs sorting out, or as a special case who needs support because of the problem.

What part do you want to play in finding the solution?

You have to decide what role you want to take. You can be part of any decisions that are made or you can hand the problem over to someone else. If you want a solution, you need to be part of the process of finding that solution because:

- you know the most about what has happened to your child
- your child will want to please you more than anyone else
- your help will be invaluable to anyone working with your child
- your involvement will be beneficial for your child because you will be learning together

HOW TO FIND A SOLUTION

Finding a solution to the problem will involve testing out ideas and exploring different possibilities. Be careful you don't lose sight of the problem you are trying to overcome. You might get side tracked and while this could give you more information you must keep remembering your goal.

Finding a solution means moving at a realistic pace.

If you follow what we suggest you should avoid the pitfalls of forgetting where your child started and not noticing the improvements she has made. Beware of spending all your time looking at what hasn't changed and thinking it's all going too slowly.

If you don't go at a realistic pace you may find your child is being labelled as having ADD as a way of experts dealing with your anxiety.

A realistic pace means taking one area you want to change, and devoting time to changing it. Don't worry about how long it seems to be taking. Every child is different.

Learning to catch a ball took Stephen three hours, Jane three weeks and Frankie one year. Learning to tie shoe laces took Stephen the whole of the school holidays, Jane two weeks and Frankie two years. Remembering her birthdate took Catherine five minutes, Philip six months and Katy fourteen months. Riding a bike took Jonathan eighteen months, Paul six weeks and Natasha one weekend.

We are not advocating that you stand back and say, 'Since all children learn things at different times, I don't need to worry if my child is different from other people and hasn't learned how to behave reasonably yet.' We are advocating that you pay attention to all the things all your children do so you can find ways of helping them all develop their potential to the full. You do not need to 'go over the top'.

A calm and relaxed approach will help you see all the options, evaluate them and decide what is the best thing for you to do.

Relaxation

HOW TO BECOME A PERSON WHO CAN GO STILL

BASIC RELAXATION TECHNIQUES

STORIES TO HELP YOU RELAX

THE IMPORTANCE OF RELAXATION

'Relaxation—what a relief!'
Relaxation is a valuable skill for everyone who wants to live life to
the full.

Why does relaxation help everyone?

Relaxation means cutting off from everyday life and going to a
point of stillness.

It means leaving the thoughts that run round and round in your
head to one side.

It means physically stopping. It means mentally stopping.

It gives everyone a break and helps them start afresh.

It helps to give protected time for the relaxation.

Can everyone relax easily?

Some people find relaxation very easy to do. Some people notice
things around them in a way that others don't. Some people see
birds in trees where other people might only see the trees. Some
people are inspired to create things all the time and they notice
other people's creations.

People who find it easy to go still, will be people who understand
how relaxation happens.

Some people who find it difficult to do a relaxation do not realise
how to go still. They will not be able to relax until they become
aware that knowing how to go still is an important part of relaxation. Then they need to realise that relaxation takes practice.

HOW TO BECOME A PERSON WHO CAN GO STILL

People who go still change the pace they were using for one activity
to a new pace. They achieve this change of pace by:

- deep breathing
- closing their eyes
- counting slowly
- thinking of something calming
- repeating a phrase or a word
- listening to music
- looking at a candle

- looking at a beautiful view and taking in the detail
- being aware of and appreciating the detail of anything they are looking at
- being aware of and appreciating the detail of anything they are listening to
- being aware of and appreciating the detail of anything they are eating
- being aware of and appreciating the detail of anything they are touching
- being aware of and appreciating the detail of something they smell

A child who looks like she will never stop fidgeting, prowls around always on a search for 'she knows not what' and never listens, can be taught to relax. Some children like this will learn how to relax very quickly. Others will take longer to realise that there is a way to be peaceful, because they have never experienced peace. This doesn't mean they live in a war zone or with an argumentative family, this just means that they haven't learned to go still in mind and body.

Jenny had terrible concentration. Her eyes would be everywhere, never stopping on one thing for more than a second. She couldn't learn because her eyes never rested on what she was being shown and her mind was never still long enough to take anything in.

Mark could not stay still. From when he got up to when he finally fell asleep he was moving. Car journeys were very difficult because he would wriggle and squirm. In school he was constantly moving around the classroom. At home, when he should have been in bed, he could be heard moving around his bedroom and the rest of the house.

Knowing how to relax is an essential skill
A child who learns to relax will learn to learn. Anyone who does not learn how to go still will not be able to plan a change from one way of living their life to another. They will not be able to learn the skills to make the change. When something is being learned it is important to go still long enough to notice how change can happen or has happened. People who don't learn to relax will find they are endlessly darting from one place to another. Their minds

will be leaping from one idea to another. They are only ever able to see something from their own point of view. It is difficult to explain to them why something needs to change. It is difficult to get them to learn anything new.

THE GIRL WHO THOUGHT SHE HAD 20/20 VISION

Karen was happy to oblige if she could see the point. The problem was she could only see the obvious and never uncover any meaning for herself. She thought what she could see was all that was available to see. If her mum said, 'Look at the cloud,' Karen would say, 'Why?'. If a teacher said, 'Turn to Chapter Two on page 37,' and Chapter Two wasn't on page 37, Karen would shut the book. If she had to look something up for her homework and she couldn't find it easily, she wouldn't explore. Everything was done mechanically—never thoughtfully. Everything was done minimally—never with any richness. It appeared Karen had no idea how to get involved at a deeper level—she always skimmed the surface. The sad thing was she thought she knew it all.

Relaxation increases the quality of thought.

BASIC RELAXATION TECHNIQUES

Before you begin any relaxation.

- Set aside a time.
- Set aside a place.
- Get comfortable (stretch out on the floor or sit comfortably with back straight and feet flat on the floor). Don't slouch or curl up.

To begin the relaxation each part of the body needs to be tensed and relaxed.

- Tighten the feet—let them go.
- Tighten the lower legs—let them go.
- Tighten the upper legs—let them go.
- Tighten the tummy—let it go.
- Tighten the chest—let it go.
- Tighten the shoulders—let them go.
- Tighten the arms—let them relax.
- Tighten the upper back—let it relax.
- Tighten the lower back—let it relax.
- Scrunch the face into a tight ball—let it relax.
- Squeeze the fingers into a tight fist—let them go.

The following relaxations can be read by you to your children. Your children can read them to themselves and you can read them for your own enjoyment and relaxation.

STORIES TO HELP YOU RELAX

A relaxation to develop observation and imagination. This relaxation will help someone who has limited imagination and can only see what is obvious to them.

I want you to imagine you are in a room that you have often been in before. You have found a doorway in this room that up until now you have never noticed. It might be behind a curtain or some furniture. It could be decorated so that it looks like part of the wall or it might be in an unusual place where you would not expect to find a doorway.

Go up to the door and turn the handle. Open the door and look inside. Inside you see that the room is all white. White ceiling, white walls and white floor. In the centre of the room is a table and on top of the table is a magnificent bowl. The bowl is the only brightly coloured thing in the room. It is a huge bowl and is in the middle of the table. The colours on the bowl are beautiful. There are rich reds, purples and crimsons, bright blues, greens and yellows. The bowl is so lovely you go over to it to see what is inside. And you find it is full of the most delicious and exotic fruit. Some fruits you have seen before but never tasted. Some fruits are your favourites. There are mangoes and pineapples, peaches and plums, strawberries and cherries. And right on the top of all the rest of the fruit is a beautiful large orange. This orange almost seems to be glowing. It looks like a sun sitting there on top of the pile.

You pick up the orange in your hand and as you do so you feel a tingle of excitement trickle up your arm from the tips of your fingers. You begin to peel the orange and as you take the skin off piece by piece you realise there is something very special about this fruit.

Inside the orange is a fantastic jewel. You put the bits of peel on the table. The jewel rests in the palm of your hand. You can feel the weight of the jewel and whether it is warm or cold. You notice its colour and how it catches the light and bounces it off round the room. You feel very special and privileged. You feel amazed and exhilarated.

Now you leave the room taking the jewel with you. You put it in your pocket or hold it in your hand. The feeling of special excitement stays with you as you close the door behind you. You will always be able to remember the pleasure you had the time you found the secret room.

A relaxation to develop a sense of perspective. This relaxation will help someone who feels overwhelmed by difficulties.

Imagine you are sitting on the bank of a river or stream. The water is fast flowing and it's a warm and sunny day. You have hardly noticed your surroundings because you have so many other things on your mind. On your lap is a notepad. This is a very special notepad because the paper from it will dissolve away as soon as it is in water. You also have a pencil. Anything written with this pencil will also disappear as soon as it touches water. You pick up the pencil and start writing. You write down on the pad all the things that have worried you lately. Things that didn't turn out the way you had hoped. Things that you were looking forward to that didn't happen and things you were dreading that did happen. You write and write. Line after line until you reach the bottom of the page. Now you rip off that page. Scrunch the page up into a ball and throw it right out into the water. Now watch as the page with your writing disappears, dissolves away.

When it has all gone you pick up the pencil again. You write about all the people who have given you a difficult time. People who have wanted you to do more than you can, people who have not understood what you wanted and people who won't leave you alone. You write it all down. Line after line and sentence after sentence until there is nothing else to write about them and you have got to the bottom of the page.

Rip out the page, scrunch it up and toss it into the water. Again watch it disappear and dissolve away in front of your eyes.

Pick up the pencil again and keep writing. All the things that have got you down, made you feel unhappy, sad or miserable are written down on the pad. Write down the things that have made you feel disappointed, lonely and hurt. Keep on writing and every time you get to the bottom of a page rip it out, scrunch it up and throw it into the water.

Finally you find you have written down everything you can think of and you have got to the end of the notepad. There are no more things to write down and all the paper has gone.

You start to notice where you are. You look around at the blue sky, the tall grasses, the birds that are by the water. You notice insects skimming across the surface of the river or stream and you can see fishes darting between the weeds. The sun is warm and the air is fresh. You drift off into a relaxed and comfortable doze. When you wake up you feel refreshed and full of energy, positive and eager to carry on with your life.

A relaxation to develop confidence. This relaxation will help someone who is feeling that a particular demand is just too difficult.

Picture yourself beginning a journey and as your journey continues you find yourself walking across a desert. You are surprised to find yourself surrounded by sand and are interested to see what will lie at the other end. As you walk you become aware of the feel of the sand beneath your feet and the heat of the air as it touches your face. As if from nowhere a wind begins to blow. At first it swirls the sand around your feet but gradually it gets stronger and you have to push your body to keep walking. You become exhausted but you keep struggling on. The sand is in your face, your eyes, your mouth. You pull your coat up round your face for protection. You realise you don't know where you are. Suddenly you stumble and fall. When you look up you see through the swirling sand a house. You stagger towards it and find a door. You have to scrape the sand from the doorway while the wind howls around you. You are determined to get in and finally manage to open the door. Once inside there is peace. You can no longer hear the wind or feel the heat. Everything is still. Everything is quiet and everything is cool. You take off your coat and begin to look around.

You see two doors—one to your left and one to your right. You open the first door and find a kitchen and you know that it is all right for you to go in. On the table, as if someone has prepared it for you, is a cool drink. You have a drink. You can feel energy returning. Now you are absolutely fascinated and you want to explore the house further. You go to the second door. You open the door and inside you find a room full of books on shelves. You step inside. On the floor is a thick carpet and two large cushions. You browse through the books. Every so often you take one off the shelf to look at it more closely. One book is so interesting you sit or lie on the cushion and begin to read. The pictures in the book are wonderful and the information is fascinating. Your mind is so full and you are so excited about what you now know. The cushions are so comfy you snuggle down and let your body stretch out and sleep. When you wake you leave the room. You notice a back door. You open it and step back out into the desert. The storm is over. In the distance you can see the sea and you know where you are. You know the memory of the storm in the desert, the peace in the house and the knowledge from the book will always stay with you.

A relaxation to develop a sense of your own past. This relaxation will help someone who feels out of touch with the past.

It is a beautiful day and you are playing on a beach. You can hear the birds and smell the salt in the air. You are happy and relaxed. You go down to the water and play at diving into the waves. You race up the beach and let the sun dry you off. You build models with the sand and carve out roads and rivers for the water. Suddenly your fingers touch something hard. It isn't a shell. You pull it out of the sand to get a better look. It is a key and you look at it carefully. It's old and rusty. You decide to take it with you and try to find the lock that it fits. Is it a key to a door? Or is it a key to a box? You don't know but you will search for the lock that it fits.

When you arrive home you take the key out and try it in all the locks you can find in the house. It doesn't fit any of the locks. You put the key away safely and every time you think there is a chance of it fitting a lock you try it.

One day you are out in the garage and you find an old wooden box. The box is locked. You remember your key and rush back into the house to get it. You try the key in the lock and it fits. With a creak the lid opens and you look inside. The box is full of photos and postcards. You take out some of the photo's and look at them. They are all of you when you were younger. Some of them might even be of you as a baby. You are fascinated to see what you used to be like, what you used to wear and the toys you used to have. You marvel at how much you have changed, at how much you know that you didn't know then and at how much you can do that you couldn't do then. You take the box inside and put it somewhere safe in your room. You decide to start a new box of photos and cards to show what you are like now and so you will always have a record of how you are changing, how you are growing and how you are learning.

A relaxation to develop a sense of realism. This relaxation will help those who never want anything to change.

It's a beautiful day and you are on a beach. You have been building something out of the sand for a long time and it really is beginning to look very special. You might have built a castle or done a sculpture of an animal. You might have made a village of little houses or made a whale out of the sand. Whatever it is you have done it looks wonderful and you are very proud of yourself for having been able to produce something as good as this. You stand back to admire your work and as you do you hear a noise. You turn round to see what is making the noise and realise it is the sea. The tide is coming in. The waves are moving up the beach and they are going to go right over your wonderful sculpture. You feel so cross and stupid at the same time. How could the sea destroy what you have worked so hard to make and how could you have forgotten about the tide? You try shouting at the waves but it makes no difference. You realise you will have to get out of the way of the water yourself.

You run up the beach and climb to the top of a cliff. From here you can watch the ocean as it engulfs your sculpture. As the tide turns and the water recedes you begin to feel a little calmer about what has happened. You look down at the place where your sculpture was and notice something half buried in the sand. You climb down the cliff and rush over to see what it is. There nestled in the sand, as if put there especially for you—just where you built your model—is the most beautiful seashell. You pick it up and look at the colours. Pinks and yellows swirling around the shell. Inside it is shiny and white. It's as if it's a gift from the sea. You take the shell with you. Now you have the memory of your creation and the memory of a beautiful shell to keep forever.

A relaxation to develop empathy and sympathy. This relaxation will help someone who is very nervous or has to deal with people who are very nervous. It also helps people who are aggressive towards others.

Picture yourself sitting on a rock that is right on the edge of the lake. It is a warm day. The lake is still and the only noise is the occasional 'plop' as a fish breaks the surface of the water.

As you sit on the rock you hear a rustling sound coming from the bushes that are just near where you are sitting. You look to see what is making the noise. The nose of your favourite creature pokes out from the leaves. Then the rest of its head appears. You can tell that the animal is frightened because its nose is twitching and it is looking around nervously. You sit as still as you can on the rock, not making a sound. Gradually the animal creeps out from the bushes and walks past where you are on the rock and goes down to the water. The animal hasn't noticed you at all and it must feel safe because when it gets down to the water it puts its head down and has a lovely long, refreshing drink from the lake.

While it drinks you look at the shape of its head, its markings, its fur or its skin, the line of its back and its tail. Finally the animal has had enough to drink. It lifts up its head and shakes off the drops of water. You stay sitting still and quiet but as it shakes its head it catches sight of you where you are on the rock. For a moment the animal is frightened. It doesn't know what to do. You stay still and keep your breathing steady. You smile at the animal and the smile and your stillness make you feel calm. The animal knows it can trust you. It slowly creeps over to the rock. If you are lucky it might climb up and sit next to you looking out over the lake. The two of you feel like friends sitting together watching. You might find you can communicate with the creature and tell it about yourself. You might find the animal talks to you about what it's been doing, thinking and feeling.

Eventually it is time for the animal to go. With one leap it gets down from the rock. You watch as it disappears back into the bush. All you can see once it has gone are the leaves moving slightly where it brushed past.

You stay sitting on the rock thinking about the special thing that has just happened—how you managed not to frighten the animal but to get it to trust you—how by staying still and quiet you made a new and unusual friend.

This relaxation will develop a sense of self worth. This relaxation helps someone who feels lost, lonely and out of place.

You are in a field playing a game with your friends. It is a game with a ball and you are enjoying throwing and catching the ball, running to find spaces and calling out to your friends. Suddenly an amazing thing happens. The ball you have been playing with bounces away and out of the game. You turn to see what is happening and you see the ball bouncing off down the field. Each time it hits the ground it changes colour. It goes from orange to red, to green, to blue. Each time it hits the floor it changes to another colour. You and your friends follow the ball. You want to find out what is happening and where it is going. You chase the ball out of the field and keep following it. After a time the ball bounces up and over a high stone wall. The wall is too high for you to be able to climb over and too high for you to be able to look over. You stand at the foot of the wall feeling disappointed and confused. But then you notice, tucked away at the bottom of the wall, a small door. You go over to the door and see that there is a key in the lock. You turn the key, push open the door and squeeze through. You find yourself in the most beautiful garden. There in the centre of the garden is a huge fountain. And held up by the water, on top of the fountain is your ball. Now the ball is a gold colour. It is held up there like a big golden sun shining out over the garden. You stand gazing at it in wonderment.

Once you have looked at the fountain you set off to explore the rest of the garden. There are ponds and streams to paddle in. There are trees to climb and caves to explore. You find fruit trees laden with fruit. You find soft grassy lawns where you can lie down for a rest and watch the clouds floating overhead. Every corner of this garden has something fascinating in it. You spend hours looking, searching and wandering through the undergrowth and the flower beds.

Finally the shadows begin to grow longer and you feel it is time to go home. The ball bounces off the fountain and back over the wall. You go out through the little door in the wall. You close the door behind you and turn the key in the lock. You pop the key into your pocket so you can return and visit this wonderful garden whenever you want.

A relaxation for developing observation. This relaxation will help someone who feels troubled to notice the fascinating things that are around them.

Imagine that as you're lying here a cloud from the sky enters the room and slides underneath you so that you are lifted up and taken out of the house as if the wall to the outside does not exist. Sometimes you lie on the cloud. Sometimes you stand on the cloud and sometimes you sit or kneel. You pass over the houses in your neighbourhood. You pass over farmland and out to the sea. Sometimes you steer your cloud so you can look at rivers and mountains in other lands. Sometimes you take your cloud up through the atmosphere and look at the stars and planets. You are struck by the wonder of the universe. Gradually you become tired and are ready to return home. You visit the places you have enjoyed most once again and then as if with no effort you find yourself back in the room where you are now. The cloud has gone. The walls are back where they were before and you have a wonderful feeling of peace and knowledge. When you are ready—open your eyes and sit up.

THE IMPORTANCE OF RELAXATION

For people who find it difficult to concentrate it is essential to learn how to relax. That way they will break the habit which has led them to have poor attention and poor ability to focus. Don't worry if it takes a long time for your child to learn how to go completely still. Even children who wriggle will gain something from the experience. By providing your child with opportunities for developing relaxation skills, you will be speeding up the learning process for your child.

By providing yourself with opportunities for developing relaxation skills, you will be speeding up the learning process for yourself.

Remember your child knows lots of people but he wants to please you most of all.

If you learn to relax you will remember to tell your child when you are pleased and your child will go on pleasing you.

All the best.

How school can help

ADVICE TO TEACHERS

ADVICE TO PARENTS

HOW TO RUN A SUCCESSFUL GROUP OUTING

WHAT YOU NEED TO CONSIDER WHEN YOU ARE HAVING
CHILDREN TO PLAY OR ORGANISING A CHILDREN'S PARTY

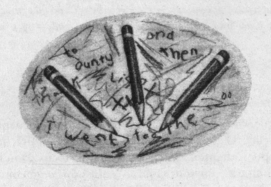

What your school can do for a child who needs to learn how to learn and learn how to let others learn.

Have clear conventions for:
- dress
- cleanliness
- equipment, pens, pencils etc.
- talking to teaching and non teaching staff
- talking to friends, classmates and peers
- presentation of work

If the conventions are blurred and low standards are accepted, then a child who hasn't learned how to behave appropriately at school, will see poor behaviour as the baseline. He will feel aggrieved if he is not allowed to behave badly because he has seen others behave like that and get away with it.

If your school has clear guidelines, parents and teachers can support each other when the child isn't conforming. This support will cut down the time you need to spend teaching the child to learn and let others learn.

Have clear procedures for talking to parents
For example—Sarah's mum and dad were sure Sarah had ADD. They came up to the school to ask the teacher what she could do about the problem. The teacher followed the school procedure.

1. She made sure all parties understood that they were there for the good of the child.
2. She made a list of things Sarah's parents felt showed Sarah had ADD. When the answers were too general she asked for more detail. For example, when the parents said Sarah was aggressive she asked when and how and to whom?
3. Then she went through the list to see if there were any points the school had already been working on and told the parents where there had been improvement in Sarah's performance.
4. Everyone looked again at the list to see if there were any other points they could begin to work on.
5. Sarah's parents were asked which points they would like to tackle with the school. Everyone agreed that it was important to choose one thing at a time so that improvement could be measured and everyone keep it as a priority. This didn't mean that other things

wouldn't be dealt with but it did mean in a busy schedule the solution to Sarah's problems wouldn't make unreasonable demands.

Points to remember when parents, teachers and others are discussing pupils.

- Identify the things that **can** be changed and list them.
- Decide from that list what people **want** to change.
- From that list decide on what it is **possible** to change.
- List the things that each person is going to be **responsible** for.
- Choose one thing that all those involved can **monitor**.
- Agree on how often you are going to meet to **check** progress.
- Don't be afraid to say the problem has or hasn't been **sorted** out.

Have clear ground rules for behaviour and clear ground rules for how poor behaviour will be managed

A rude child needs to learn respect and so needs to see respect given and expected by staff and pupils at all appropriate times. This will mean that when this standard is varied the child will have some chance of understanding why.

A disaffected child has little understanding that the way he's behaved at one time affects the way people behave towards him later.

A child who is not concentrating has little understanding that his effort will affect his performance. Everything just happens and if he is not the focus of attention then he thinks he has no reason to behave in the way everybody else is. Then he feels entitled to be aggrieved when he is treated differently.

You sometimes find an adult who doesn't want the child to get better. If one expert says the child is making good progress and no longer needs to be singled out for special treatment, those adults will look for a new expert who will agree with their view.

ADVICE TO TEACHERS

If you have a parent who is constantly on the telephone telling you how worried he is because his child isn't succeeding, ask him for one thing that would make him feel more positive about the child's progress. Teach the child that thing.

For most parents goalposts in education are very hard to set.

They know that their children should be literate and numerate and able to look after themselves, but they are unsure of what their realistic expectations should be.

If they set the goal and their child can be helped to achieve it you have demonstrated.

- that you have taken them seriously
- you know how to teach
- their child knows how to learn

Where a parent doesn't respond to this you may have to accept there is nothing else you can do. For some teachers this is very painful because they have committed so much time and effort to helping the child and in some cases the whole family. It can feel as if all the effort and commitment has been discounted. Remember you don't have to win them all, just a reasonable percentage. A 100 per cent success rate would be great but somewhere over 80 per cent is more realistic.

ADVICE TO PARENTS

The suggestions above work just as well if it is a teacher on the telephone saying he is worried about your child.

PARENTS AND TEACHERS WORKING TOGETHER

Emily had just started secondary school and within weeks had been banned from every school visit. She was not allowed to go swimming, visit the library or go to the theatre and she was certainly not going to be taken away with the school for the weekend. Emily and her mother were devastated. Emily's parents had taken her on many visits and she had never embarrassed them. It had seemed to them that Emily loved outings. Emily could be difficult in many other situations but if they were on excursions, they thought Emily behaved very well. Emily's parents went up to the school to explain their position but the school was adamant that Emily would not be allowed to join in until she had learned not to be disruptive and a danger to the group. They told the parents that on school trips Emily would constantly wander off and unless someone was allocated to her she would get lost. She would often flounce about so things were knocked over and broken. Emily wanted to be accepted on school trips so she and her parents sat down and made a list of what the school needs Emily to be able to do.

1. Look pleasant when she is out with the school and look interested when someone is talking to the group.
2. Move carefully so she doesn't knock into other people or into things around her.
3. Ask questions in a clear voice and then listen to the answer.
4. Take responsibility for staying with the group.
5. Take note of the time she is expected to be ready and the time she is expected to be back on the bus.

Has your child been banned?

If you have a child who has been banned from activities and is causing concern you may find the school suggests that experts should be brought in. You can take the initiative by teaching your child whatever hasn't been understood. Start by making a list. After you've made the list see if a friend or relative will check the list to make sure all the areas you need to cover are covered.

Sometimes people are too embarrassed to tell you what they really think about your child's behaviour, but a list helps make it less awkward. It lessens the feeling that someone is making a personal attack rather than offering help.

Now ask the school to check the list. Some people feel that parents are unable to help their children if something has gone wrong and it is true that parents are often too close to be able to see where the problem is. But it does not follow that parents can not help.

Emily was so successful learning how to behave, that she was able to visit her mother's friend's family in Japan. Emily travelled alone, went to an international school for a month and achieved high grades. When she returned, her marks continued to improve but the school still needed convincing that she was safe enough for them to lift the ban. To Emily and her parents it seemed that Emily had proved herself, but from the school's position Emily could still put other children or staff in jeopardy. Emily had to be patient and when the class went to a park for a geography lesson, she had the opportunity to show that she could be trusted.

How to Run a Successful Group Outing

Points to consider.

1. If you have children in the group who find it difficult to behave in a responsible way have practice outings. These outings should be to places where you don't have to involve other people or paying money such as going to the park or to the museum because:
   - you shouldn't feel under pressure to struggle on with the activity because you have paid or arranged for other people to be there
   - a trip which has cost money for everyone, shouldn't turn into a behaviour modification exercise for one child
   - a trip which has cost money for everybody shouldn't be sacrificed in order to teach a lesson to one child

2. You can run a program which involves all the children in a group by having different activities available. Children will be selected for an activity if they have sufficient skill to make it enjoyable. To overcome embarrassment you could present it to the parents as:
   - if your child can walk two miles he can come to the park
   - if your child can move around in a confined space he can come to the library
   - if your child can understand the dangers cliffs present he can come for a walk along the coastal path
   - if your child will always come when he is called and can walk sensibly as part of a group, he can come on the midnight walk

   A list like this helps parents know what they can practise or discuss with their children. (Children who need more support because of physical or other difficulties should be allowed to come and provision made for them so the trip is enjoyable for everyone.)

3. Let the parents know the role you need them to play. They could prepare their children with:
   - questions
   - appropriate clothing—you may need to tell the parents what that is
   - appropriate food following your stated policy

4. Parents need to:
   - drop children off on time and in a state of readiness for the trip
   - collect children on time—it may be better to be there five minutes early than five minutes late

• talk to their children about the trip before and after—you might find it useful to prepare a list of questions for parents to ask the children.

Preparing for excursions

What parents and teachers need to teach children before a class visit to a library. A class visit is quite different from a family visit to a library although some of the rules will be the same.

1. Walk quietly.
2. Stay together.
3. Don't disturb other library users or get in their way when they are looking at books.
4. There will be no time to go to the toilet during the visit but there will be a toilet stop before the visit begins.
5. Children should come with a list of questions that would be suitable for them to ask.

A Note to Librarians

1. Send a letter to the school before a class visit. This letter should detail what you need the children to know and how many helpers you recommend coming with the children.
2. You can suggest to the teacher or adult leader of any group that this letter can form the basis of the first lesson about the library and that lesson should happen before the group visit.
3. Once the group has arrived make sure you begin with a review of what is in the letter. Ask the children:
   • what they think walk quietly means
   • why they think they mustn't disturb anyone
   • how people might be disturbed
   and so on.

If you think the children have not been briefed by the teacher, use the time of the visit to do the briefing and arrange a time for another visit. Remember you are responsible for everyone in the library as well as the visiting group.

Note: Children need to know it is a privilege to go on a visit. It may be part of a course but there will be expectations that the children will contribute positively to the experience. If you have an ADD child, whether you are a parent or a teacher, and that child is likely to disrupt a class trip, you can use the above list to practise with him how to go on a visit.

WHAT YOU NEED TO CONSIDER WHEN YOU ARE HAVING CHILDREN TO PLAY OR ORGANISING A CHILDREN'S PARTY

1. The first thing you have to decide is what support you need from the children in order for the event to work at all.
2. Then you need to decide what you want the children to have achieved from the activity.
3. Are you going to do all the preparation before and clear up after or are you going to find parts of the activity where the children can help.

HOW ONE PARTY WENT WRONG

Annabel's mum was very excited that Annabel had asked if she could have a birthday party at home. She had six friends whom she wanted to come to tea. Annabel's mum remembered her best party as a child and began to plan. She made little cardboard baskets to put sweets in. She blew up balloons and made them into festive bunches. Annabel's dad was away on business but hoped to be back for the last hour of her party. Annabel's mum knew everything. She knew what they were going to do and when they were going to do it. Unfortunately she hadn't realised what children can be like when they are in a group. She didn't realise she would need to tell the children where they could go in the house and where they could not. She didn't realise she would have to tell them not to open cupboards. She thought that since they were all friends they would be nice to each other. Sadly the party of Annabel's mum's dreams did not happen.

Instead she had mayhem.

Annabel's dad came home to find a white lipped wife, his own child sent to bed, four children in front of the television and one locked in the bathroom refusing to come out. There were muddy footprints all over the living room floor because the children had devised a hide and seek game which ranged in and out of the house.

The ground rules for planning a children's party and avoiding 'ADD-like' behaviour are as follows.

1. Have treats but make sure there is some sensible food all the children will eat. Encourage parents to tell you which foods their children react badly to—orange squash etc. and avoid them.
2. Make sure there is a suitable place for the children to sit down and eat.
3. Make sure all the children know exactly where they can go. Tell them where the toilets are and decide if they are allowed to lock the door.
4. Make sure you, or other adults who understand what you want and are prepared to be on duty, are around all the time in case the children need your help to sort out problems—accidents, disputes or requests.
5. Make sure any noisy event is in your control. Many children feel a party has been successful if they have had the chance to be noisy as well. If you feel it is getting out of control—stop it.
6. Every successful party will have moments where the children come together to do something focused—singing Happy Birthday or playing pass the parcel.
7. It is better to leave something out you think might have been fun rather than risk turning the party into a nightmare.

Support groups

Support groups have different roles. They are there to educate the public as well as their members.

THEY MAY:
- try to help people see that they can sort the problem out for themselves
- exist to put pressure on the authorities to provide compensatory help
- provide a place where people can talk about their problem

Some support groups give you an understanding of what you can do next to overcome the problem completely. They may help you find ways of ensuring that you are doing everything possible to help yourself. These groups typically have speakers who are offering ways of being successful. They encourage debate and a variety of approaches.

Problems with concentration and behaviour can tie the child and the family in knots. A real tangle can be gently picked at until one bit is loosened and the problem begins to be manageable. Energy which had gone in frustration and despair is able to be used to look at the next area which might be sorted out. The family begins to feel they can cope and the child gains confidence that he can be parented like everyone else.

Some support groups will prop you up but may make you feel that membership of the group depends on you recognising that the problem will never go away. These groups will look to the authorities and the public to offer sympathy and help. They will typically have speakers who reinforce the message that the condition is chronic.

Some groups will drag you down. Here you will be asked your problem and you will be told the problems of the others in the group. You may end up feeling you are desperately unfortunate to be afflicted. The purpose of the group will be to listen and share experiences of the problem rather than try out and share possible solutions. Typical speakers at these groups will be able to talk of their misery but not of their triumphs.

It is helpful to think what sort of a group you want to join.

- Do you want it to be complaining or explaining?
- Do you want it to emphasise self help?
- Do you want open discussion?
- Do you want to be given detailed explanations on getting help from the authorities?

It is worth checking the following.

- Where does the group get its finances from?
- Who is on the committee?
- What sort of speakers do they have?
- What do they put in their publicity?

After you have been to one meeting you will know more about the group.

- Are they a listening or a telling group?
- Do you feel hopeful or hopeless?
- Do they describe children as if the label sums them up completely, for example I've got an ADD child; my child is a dyslexic; my child is an 'Aspergers.'
- Do they describe children who have overcome the problem.

Here are some things to check before you join the group.

- What does it costs to join?
- What will you get for your money?
- Is there another group that meets at a more convenient time, a more convenient place or offers a creche?

Don't feel intimidated by a group. You are not letting your child down if you have a different view from everyone else. You have the right to ask questions.

There is advice in this book for dealing with experts. The same advice can also be helpful when you are looking for a support group.